The publication staff of this book would like to extend
their appreciation to National City Bank,
formerly First of America Bank, for their support
and sponsorship of the initial printing of
Springfield Entertainment: A Pictorial History,
the second in a series of four books on Springfield's
history. Such efforts to record and preserve
Springfield's rich traditions greatly
benefit the present and future citizens of our
community. We also wish to express our heartfelt
thanks to all those who have contributed to this
outstanding reflection of our heritage.

Springfield Entertainment

A PICTORIAL HISTORY

by

Curtis Mann
Edward Russo
Melinda Garvert

Photographs from the
Sangamon Valley Collection
Lincoln Library

G. Bradley Publishing
St. Louis, Missouri 63131

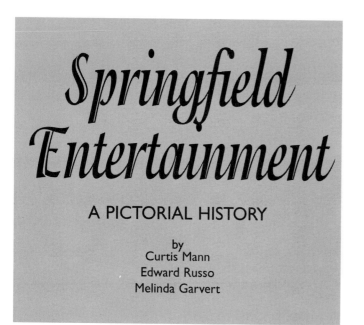

Springfield Entertainment

A PICTORIAL HISTORY

by
Curtis Mann
Edward Russo
Melinda Garvert

PUBLICATION STAFF:
Authors: Curtis Mann, Edward Russo,
and Melinda Garvert
Cover Artist: Betty Madden-Work
Book Design: Diane Kramer
Photo Editor: Michael Bruner
Copy Editor: William Furry
Publisher: G. Bradley Publishing, Inc.
Sponsor: National City Bank

Table of Contents

Reprint 1998

ISBN-0-943963-55-9
PRINTED IN THE UNITED STATES OF AMERICA

Foreword

It follows that a community that works well together, plays well together. Springfield is no exception, having both a rich tradition of getting things done and having fun at the same time.

From the city's earliest days its citizens have sought entertainment after the day's work was done. The rude pleasures of the prairie pioneers—corn husking, cabin raising, horse racing, barn dancing (activities usually lubricated with a plentiful supply of whisky)—later gave way to more temperate recreation, such as organized sporting events, bicycle clubs, debating societies, social clubs, and theater and ballet companies. In the last century the advent of motion pictures, radio and television, and most of all, the automobile, drastically changed the way people played.

This book, volume two in a four-part series that began with *Springfield Business: A Pictorial History*, looks at those formative years when Springfieldians and, indeed, all Americans found themselves with more leisure time. Luckily for us the ingenious ways they filled their time were captured by the camera's lens, which gives us this opportunity to share in the fun. We are all indebted to the countless and often-anonymous photographers who took these pictures. While the earlier volume captured Springfield at work, Springfield Entertainment documents the community at play. As in the previous volume, all photographs, unless noted, are from Lincoln Library's Sangamon Valley Collection, which owns thousands of photographs of Springfield and central Illinois scenes.

Unfortunately, this collection represents only a fraction of the diverse recreation-related activities, organizations, and events that have amused citizens in this community since its founding more than 170 years ago. And while we regret the representation depicted herein is not all-inclusive, we celebrate what has been recovered, and hope it will inspire others to share their histories and photos with future generations.

We hope you enjoy this brief look back at our history at its most relaxed.

Sugar Bowl Restaurant circa 1940.

In pre-Civil War Springfield, entertainment and recreation were important for the residents of Springfield. Life in the small community was hard and every opportunity to gather together socially was enthusiastically received. Early forms of entertainment in Springfield were numerous, many focused on a purpose. Cabin-raisings, corn-huskings, cotton-pickings and communal wolf hunts for example, were purposeful, but they were also a time for people to enjoy being with others. Events such as weddings and religious camp meetings were times when people gathered to eat and dance (or worship). Whiskey was routinely on hand to be served to thirsty participants at most events. Springfield had several taverns to provide food and drink to people who met to talk and socialize. Audiences gathered to listen to proceedings on the days when the court was in session. Fourth of July celebrations included parades, dinners, and toasts. Horse racing, cards and other forms of gambling were popular. The first race track was reported to be near Hall & Herrick's store, which stood on the east side of the public square and was later moved a mile south, across South Grand Avenue. Horse racing was very popular on the frontier and Springfield had its fair share of racers. Many were impromptu affairs where two riders meeting on a street would challenge each other and

The Cirque De Hippodrome was one of at least three traveling circuses that performed in Springfield in 1855. Circuses were a common form of entertainment throughout most of Springfield's existence. Admission was fifty cents for adults and twenty-five cents for children to attend one of the four shows. The "Bear Woman" was touted as a main feature of the show.

"How much Springfield is improving, is the general remark of strangers, on coming into the place. The introduction of gas is a very great improvement, all the principal streets are lit and we wonder how we ever navigated, through the mud, without it. There will be no legislature this winter and I suppose the city will not be very gay but just now, there is no lack of amusements in the way of lectures and concerts. Reverend H.W. Beecher and the blind preacher (William Henry) Milburn and others have been lecturing and will return soon. Julian and Balti have given one concert and will give another tomorrow night. Dempster has been here and the Hutchinsons and Campbells are coming."

Louisa Iles Carter letter to her brother Thomas Iles. 1855

Corn-huskings were appealing occasions for pioneers. Often contests were made out of the event with two teams racing each other to see who could shuck their pile of corn first. After the work was done, eating and dancing occurred to close out the evening.

meet at the edge of town for a match. Swimming was done in the numerous ponds and creeks that surrounded the city. In winter these same waterways provided a place for ice skating. Sledding was a winter-time sport enjoyed by many.

As Springfield grew, more citified entertainments arrived. Many of these no longer served any obvious useful purpose. By the mid-1830s a circus had visited, military companies formed and a Thespian Society was organized. The society's first production was "The Charcoal Burner" in 1836. Hunting remained a popular pastime. R.W. Diller noted that "deer and turkey were quite plenty in any of the timber within three miles of the town, and with hounds, hunters could have a chase any day." The removal of the state capital from Vandalia to Springfield greatly enhanced the recreation opportunities. The population of Springfield swelled as people from across the state came to the city when the legislature was in assembly. Dances, dinner parties and political speeches were enjoyed by many people during the legislative "season".

> *"Of the deep snow of 1830 and '31, I...remember it lasted a long time and have a vivid recollection of the pleasure we boys had with our little handsleds, sliding down the hills and hitching on to the sleighs and sleds going along the streets. Sometimes there would be as many as a dozen strung after one sleigh."*
>
> "Description of Springfield" by Zimri Enos, Publication no. 14, Illinois State Historical Society

Camp meetings were another occasion that drew large crowds of people. As noted by R. Carlyle Burley in his book *The Old Northwest Pioner Period,* "a large element of the population enjoyed them. They served as picnics; they furnished excitement and offered emotional outlets."

Built on the east side of the public square in 1858, Cook's Hall was the largest amusement place in Springfield. As noted by John C. Cook, son of the builder John Cook, there were shown "many interesting entertainments, among them the panorama of "Dr. Kane's Arctic Expedition," Colonel Tom Thumb, Commodore Nutt, and Minnie and Lavinia Warren."

Clear Lake Hotel

This 1890s photo shows one of the cabins erected at the lake, which was used by fishing clubs, campers and picnickers. Many private sports clubs kept places out on the lake.

"Clear Lake is now fitted up in the best of style. Mr. J.H. Patterson is prepared to provide all kinds of refreshments, ice cream, lemonade, cakes, oranges & c. for picnic parties and all those who may visit this beautiful place for health or pleasure. He has also fitted up a fine sailboat for the benefit of the pleasure seekers."

Illinois State Journal,
June 30, 1858

"The Clear Lake Hotel was built by Mr. Chapman, of our city and is situated in a pretty grove bordering on the lake. It is a neat looking building two stories high..."
"The room he has reserved for dancing on the first floor, being 24 by 80 feet. The house is fitted up in good style, making it the very place to go for enjoyment."

Illinois State Journal,
June 18, 1859

The Clear Lake Hotel was built in the late 1850s by Springfield merchant Joseph Chapman and his father-in-law, John H. Patterson. It was a popular summer recreation spot for several decades. It served as an officers' quarters during the Civil War when Camp Butler was first opened. This illustration from the 1874 Sangamon County Atlas shows the Clear Lake Hotel and grounds (looking east).

"Clear Lake is a beautiful sheet of water, about one-half mile in length and on average width of 200 yards. On the banks of this lake, many picnic parties are held each summer, and boats are provided for sailing and rowing upon the lake."

History of Sangamon County, Illinois, *1881, page 851.*

"Clear Lake is a narrow sheet of water about half a mile in length, on the east side of the Sangamon and running parallel with that stream. Buildings have been erected for accommodation of visitors as resorts and it is the center of numerous picnic parties from Springfield and vicinity during the summer months. It is reached by a suburban car-line and during the past few years a series of successful chautauqas have been held there."

Historical Encyclopedia of Illinois and History of Sangamon County, *Newton Bateman and Paul Selby Editors, 1912, page 708.*

Elections, especially presidential elections, were times of parades and much fanfare. The log cabin and hard-cider campaign of 1840 was noted by historian Paul Angle as "the rowdiest, noisiest presidential campaign in the history of the country." William Henry Harrison, the hero of the battle of Tippecanoe, was the Whig candidate and his Democratic opponent was Martin Van Buren. A huge rally of Whigs on the 2nd through the 4th of June in Springfield featured a large parade with delegations from different counties. Many contingents brought cabins on wheels drawn by horse and oxen while others had canoes and hard-cider barrels. Thousands of people attended the rally to enjoy the speeches and barbecues. Harrison eventually won the election, carrying Springfield by two-thirds of the vote.

The arrival of railroads in Springfield improved transportation to the city and with them came numerous lecturers, musicians, theatrical groups, and other entertainers who filled the new public auditoriums such as the Metropolitan Hall on the corner of Third and Jefferson streets and Cook's Hall on the east side of the public square. A state fair was organized bringing more visitors to Springfield. In the years since, Springfield has enjoyed nationally known entertainers, movies, hobbies, fads, and fashions popular throughout the rest of the country.

"During the early sixties ice skating was one of the great amusements for the young people of the town. The favorite spot was Robinson's Lake...about three miles northwest of Springfield. It was here that Wirt Butler, Morris Starne, Will Bunn, the Campbells and many more displayed their skill. After a few years the progressive citizens of Springfield erected a large covered skating rink on the southwest corner of Walnut and Capital Avenue. This was largely patronized by the young people. Many tournaments were held there and some of the finest professional skaters were brought here for exhibitions. The music for the entertainments was furnished by Butler's band, which was the only brass band in Springfield."

John C. Cook, Reminiscences of Springfield, *Illinois State Journal*, March 6, 1927.

Boating was a passion for many pleasure seekers who went out on the water to fish, sightsee, or just take a relaxing tour of the lake.

Hunting was a pastime enjoyed by many men, boys and even some women. Harvested grain fields on the edge of town were excellent places for city dwellers to shoot game such as fowl, rabbit and deer. These two unidentified men are preparing to hunt in such a field.

Chapter 2: Springfield Naturally

Outdoor activities have always been popular forms of recreation in Springfield. Activities include swimming, fishing, and picnicking in the summer; hunting or hiking in the fall, and sledding and skating in the winter. Boating was popular on the Sangamon River and in the lagoons of Springfield's parks. Cycling along the city's streets became popular in the 1890s. Athletic fields provided sites for city teams and visitors to compete in baseball and football games. Golf courses gradually attracted large numbers of players. Families whiled away their afternoons playing yard games like croquet and badminton.

A heavy, wet snowfall such as this scene from the 1920s just outside of Springfield could make travel difficult. However, such snowfall provided many opportunities for winter recreational activities—sledding, skiing, and sleighing.

Snow Bounding

Snowball fights were not just for children, as this photo of a group of adults reveals. This snow battle took place in Springfield's Reservoir Park, circa 1918.

Children have ever been attracted to snow. One of the pleasurable activities associated with snow was building forts and waging "war" against one another. This group of Springfield children stand proudly above their snow fort, complete with an American flag. The photo was taken about 1910 in front of the J. Elmer Gard home at 612 Black Avenue.

The lagoon at Washington Park provided a place for boating and fishing in the warm months of the year and an excellent location for ice skating during winter. Several skaters glide across the ice in this 1907 photo.

All across Springfield frozen ponds and other waterways allowed skating enthusiasts to pursue their passion. The frozen expanse of Lake Springfield in the winter of 1939-40 was an ideal spot for skaters.

Frozen water on the tennis courts of Iles Park made an impromptu skating rink for the neighborhood children.   Skaters, sledders, and even a bicyclist amuse themselves in this 1938 photo.

Swimming Holes

Going for a swim was almost a foreign thought for pre-1900 Springfield city dwellers. A farmer's pond, or a deep spot in a creek or Sangamon River slough provided the few opportunities to cool off in the summer. The men shown here have found such a location along the Sangamon River, circa 1900.

This group of young ladies has found a swimming hole of their own. One woman prepares to dive off a homemade diving board while her companions observe from the bank and from the boats.

Springfield opened its first public swimming pool on June 16, 1928, by dedicating it to the Soldiers and Sailors of the United States, 1776, 1812, 1848, 1861, 1898 and 1917. The noted architectural firm of Helmle and Helmle designed Soldiers and Sailors Memorial Pool with a great concern for sanitary conditions. Swimmers were provided sterilized towels and swimsuits and had to pass thru showers and a foot bath before getting to the pools. (Photo about 1928)

Bathers enjoy the cool waters of Lake Springfield while others crowd the beach-house in this late 1930s photo. Many more are taking in the sun on the beach.

Located at Ninth and Converse streets, Soldiers and Sailors Memorial Pool was actually two pools, one for adults, the other for children. By 1974 maintenance costs, the change of the neighborhood to commercial uses, and poor revenues finally forced the closing of the pools, which provided so many hours of fun and relief from the summer's heat in the pre-home air conditioner days. (Photo 1960)

Lake Springfield – Playground of Central Illinois

Unlike many man-made lakes built as reservoirs, Lake Springfield from the planning stages was designed to meet not only the city's anticipated water needs but also to provide recreation. In 1930, voters readily approved both the construction of the lake and a bond referendum to build it. Fortunately, property-tax monies were not needed as revenues from the water department were sufficient for construction.

Wisely, the city kept ownership of all of the marginal land around the lake and set up a plan that parceled out leases to prospective homeowners, clubs, and camps, retaining 60 percent of the land and about half of the shoreline for public use. When the lake is full, there are 57 miles of shoreline and 6.8 square miles of water for swimmers, boater, skiers and fishermen to enjoy. Public use of lands include picnic parks, a golf course, a public beach, boat launches, zoo, a garden, and wildlife sanctuary.

Whether sailing, motoring, or rowing, Lake Springfield has offered many hours of pleasure to families, such as the Paul S. Penewitts, pictured in photo at left. Penewitt was one of the charter members of the Island Bay Yacht Club, which has held the annual Middle States Championship Regatta since 1939.

The "playground of central Illinois," as the lake has been called, was begun in 1932, and, despite a drought, filled with water that spilled over the Spaulding Dam for the first time on May 2, 1935. This late 1930s view of the lake shows the Spaulding Dam and East Lake Drive.

Boats on Lake Springfield come in all shapes and sizes. This working towboat just passed under Lindsay Bridge, but pleasure boats dominate the lake. There were once two large excursion boats brought from the 1933 World's Fair offering tours of the lake.

This view from an inlet of the lake shows some of the private homes built along the much-coveted shoreline property.

Island Bay Yacht Club, shown in this 1950s photo, is representative of many clubs that lease property at the lake. Some belong to specific organizations such as the YMCA or the Disabled American Veterans, while others are established to meet the interests of their members. The Springfield Motor Boat Club is the oldest, organizing in 1933 before the lake was even completed.

Official Program

LAKE SPRINGFIELD
BOAT
REGATTA
SUNDAY, JULY 30TH 1939

AT
LAKE
PARK

SANCTIONED BY
MID-WEST POWER BOAT ASSOCIATION

Conveniently located near Springfield and centrally located in the state, Lake Springfield offers a variety of activities to the general public.

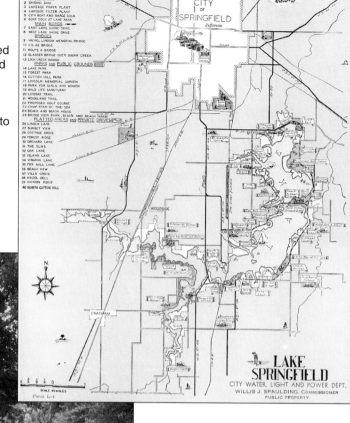

Part of the lake's public lands are used for parks— East Forest, West Forest, Cotton Hill, Bridgeview. Picnicing has always been a popular activity, followed by ball games, horseshoes, or just relaxing and enjoying a breeze off the lake. These young people are taking advantage of a day at Center Park in the 1950s.

Initially there were two public beaches, one at Lake Park for whites and the other at Bridgeview Park for blacks (Bridgeview Beachhouse is pictured.) These two beaches were segregated until 1952. The expense of maintaining the two beaches finally closed the Bridgeview facility in 1972.

Parks of Springfield

A shady grove was always a welcome gathering spot in the pioneer days of Springfield. Whether for a political rally, a religious camp meeting, or a Fourth of July picnic, Springfield had several "groves" popular with crowds. Zimri Enos recognized the desire for park-like places and in 1836, donated the town's first-known park. That small park, near the Town Branch, was called Lanphier Park, and was along today's Salome Street. This Lanphier Park, however, had no organized government maintenance and soon became a dumping ground—a common problem for several later parks donated to the city. This, combined with the increased pressures of urbanization, provoked the citizens to petition and vote for the creation of a park district.

In February of 1900, the newly-created Springfield Pleasure Driveway and Park District began developing four major parks in each cardinal direction of the city. The plan was to provide neighborhood "breathing spaces" and include a system of pleasure driveways between the major parks. The Park District was also in charge of city street trees, but maintaining streets soon proved too expensive for the district and were unceremoniously returned to the city in the 1930s. Outer Park Drive is one section of the Pleasure driveway system that is reminiscent of the original plan.

The four major parks, Washington, Lincoln, Bunn and Bergen, were all acquired by 1912. The noted landscape designer Ossian Cole Simonds was hired to plan and consult on the parks and driveway layouts. The development of the neighborhood parks was slower, due to the cost of these major parks. Enos, Matheny, Forest and Furniture Factory were some of the earliest neighborhood parks. Enos Park was donated by Zimri's sister, Susan, to honor their father and mother, Pascal and Salome, who were partners with Elijah Iles in purchasing the land for the original town.

Enjoying the quiet pleasure of an afternoon by the pond in Washington Park were several ladies in the large picture photographed in 1902. Parks are for fun is well-demonstrated by these teachers from DuBois School as they pose on a slide in Lincoln Park (inset) in 1920.

Washington Park

In the early 1890s lumber merchant Henry Schuck and brewer George Reisch laid out a 17.5-acre park at the west end of the South Grand Avenue streetcar line complete with concrete duck ponds. In 1900 after the founding of the new Pleasure Driveway and Park District, that park was incorporated into the new, larger Washington Park. Leading landscape designer Ossian C. Simonds set about designing curved drives, naturalistic landscaping, and plantings. The park was so well preserved it was named to the National Register of Historic Places in 1992.

Water from the mineral spring in Washington Park was at one time sold at the Leland Hotel, and believed to have therapeutic properties. The public health department capped the spring in the 1960s.

The aesthetic appeal of the rustic bridges built in both Washington and Lincoln parks began to give away to the more practical concrete bridges after 1910.

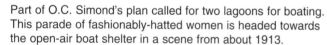

Two young women enjoy a warm spring day on a hill behind the pavilion that was built in 1903.

Part of O.C. Simond's plan called for two lagoons for boating. This parade of fashionably-hatted women is headed towards the open-air boat shelter in a scene from about 1913.

The wading pools at both Washington (shown here) and Lincoln parks were immensely popular with young children. They were one of the early recreational additions to the newly created parks.

Girls and boys competed in the annual Jaycee's Fishing Rodeos in the 1950s. Prizes for both the largest and smallest fish were awarded.

The fishing contests at Washington Park in the 1950s were well-attended. Poles and lines only were permitted: No rods and reels allowed!

21

Iles Park

Iles Park is a fitting tribute to founder, Elijah Iles, who greatly enjoyed life out-of-doors. He had a special appreciation for wooded areas, having nurtured an oak grove on his farm and planted many trees elsewhere. An eulogy for Iles noted "here are many marks to perpetuate his memory—stately trees of a half a century trace their births to his hands..." Iles Park, was in a sense, donated by the Springfield founder. Elijah Iles' will allowed his estate executors the discretion to subdivide his land and to donate public streets and parks in his name. About 1885, the city accepted 10.5 acres for a park south of South Grand between Sixth and Ninth streets. It remained undeveloped, though, until the city turned it over to the park board in 1903, making it the second public park for the new board.

(The park shared in a bit of Springfield history as it was used as the first campsite of the misfortunate Reed /Donner Party after they organized a wagon train in 1846.)

Parks have often been used as places to memorialize people or events. Here J.R. Fitzpatrick, far right, dedicates a flagpole he has given to Iles Park in memory of his son, Jim, who died in 1946. Also pictured in this 1965 photo are (left to right) Robert Stuart, Louis Gietl, Philip Robinson, Robert Lawson and John J. Watt.

When people see a stone building in Springfield, James S. Culver and his stone construction business come to mind. He built this small pavilion, pictured here in 1915. It provided a refreshment stand for hundreds of people attending ballgames, concerts, hometown talent shows, and other activities held in Iles Park.

Bunn Park

A private park, Mildred Park, became the nucleus of land for present-day Bunn Park. Mildred Park had several glory years as a private amusement park before bankruptcy caused its sale. The original park centered around the lagoon in present Bunn Park. The Park District purchased the bankrupt Mildred Park and additional land and established a new park in 1912. It was renamed to honor John W. Bunn.

Bunn came to Springfield as a teenager from New Jersey in 1847 to work in his brother Jacob's grocery business. John W. Bunn became a highly successful businessman in his own right. It was, however, his generosity and involvement with community projects that inspired the park board to name the park for him.

While swimming was allowed in some muddy-bottomed park lagoons, Bunn Park had Springfield's first public beach. It took the park board some time to negotiate with the city to re-route a sewer before the beach project could be accomplished, but as can be seen in this circa-1918 picture, the efforts were well-appreciated.

As winding roadways were first being designed for the parks, there was discussion of whether or not to allow automobiles. A speed limit was established for horses and bicyclists: eight miles per hour. As seen in this 1922 view, roads and bridges were soon prepared to handle automobile traffic.

By 1912 the Springfield Pleasure Driveway and Park Board had begun discussions about creating a public golf course. Regarding Bunn Park, their annual report commented: "The ground is admirably adapted for the purpose, and could be laid out as a golf course without any great expenditure for artificial bunkers and hazards." The picture is a circa 1916 view.

The Knights of Columbus annual barbecue, shown here in 1922 on the Sacred Heart Convent grounds, is just one example of large picnics organized by clubs, churches, organizations, associations, and especially companies. Allis-Chalmers, Sangamo Electric, CIPS, and other companies had annual employee picnics as a way to foster goodwill among managers and staff.

Swenson Photo

25

Lincoln Memorial Garden

Created from farmland that became shoreline for Lake Springfield, Lincoln Memorial Garden was skillfully planted to resemble various wooded and prairie habitats that pioneer Abraham Lincoln would have encountered. Despite its natural appearances of all seventy-seven-plus acres, the garden is cultivated, weeded and tended. In 1932, as plans for the new lake began, Mrs. Harriet Knudson approached Mayor John Kapp and Commissioner of Public Property Willis J.

Spaulding with her idea of a living memorial to Lincoln. With their approval, Mrs. Knudson gained the support of the Garden Clubs of Illinois as sponsors of the project and the famed landscape architect Jens Jensen as designer. Jensen donated his services to what has since been called one of his greatest works. Garden clubs across the nation contributed funds, giving it a national significance for all who enjoy its beauty.

Camera enthusiasts, nature lovers, hikers—all visitors to the Garden—can find the natural colors of each season enhanced by the arranged plantings, whether it be the groves of specific trees, a marshy area of moisture-loving plants or a prairie meadow.

DOGWOOD LANE – ABRAHAM LINCOLN MEMORIAL GARDEN, Springfield, Ill.

Jens Jensen (center) explains his vision of the land reserved for the first living memorial to Abraham Lincoln to Mrs. Harriet Knudson and her husband, Dr. T.J. Knudson.

One of the larger birthday presents ever given to Mrs. Charles R. Walgreen from her husband, the drugstore owner, was this seventy-five-foot bridge in Lincoln Memorial Garden. Mrs. Walgreen of Dixon, Illinois, was very active in the Garden Clubs of Illinois, which raised money to construct the garden.

Lincoln Park

Oak Ridge Park was well-known to Springfieldians in the last half of the 1800s. The Capital City Railroad Company, a streetcar line, owned the park adjacent to Oak Ridge Cemetery. It had set up a pagoda for refreshments, provided "pure well-water," and "seats under most every tree" for those seeking a day's outing. It was in this Oak Ridge Park that inventor A.L. Ide demonstrated the first electric lights (arc lights) in Springfield in the winter of 1879-80. The private twelve-acre Oak Ridge Park was donated to the newly formed Springfield Park District in 1904. By 1905, the Park District had acquired the additional land it wanted, making a new eighty-eight-acre park re-named for Abraham Lincoln.

The pagoda in the old Oak Ridge Park where refreshments were served was a focal point for those who came to picnic, enjoy the croquet grounds, listen to speakers, or allow their children to use the playground equipment. During the 1870s and '80s, the fenced off area was a popular walkers' race track with prizes and betting allowed. As Lincoln Park, athletic fields continued to be a notable feature of the park. Photo 1884.

Built in 1911 the stone bridge became a prominent element of Lincoln Park. Its sculptured design mirrors itself in the still water of the lagoon and provides a tranquil view from the stone pavilion above.

The Lincoln Inn, as the pavilion was known in its early days, was fitted with a kitchen, dining room, and soda fountain in the lower level. Dances were held on the main level.

"Rezzy" is what some of the Northenders called Reservoir Park, located where Lanphier High School is today. Small lagoons and lakes were created in the building of the seventy-five-foot-high reservoir, which held Springfield's emergency water supply. The park opened in the early 1870s with boating, tennis courts, croquet grounds, flower gardens, and picnic areas.

Reservoir Park

Reservoir Park was the only developed city-owned park before the park district was formed. It provided year-round activities. There are those who still remember a toboggan ride down the side of the reservoir, a picnic in the shade of its trees, or a boat ride in among the ducks and swans. The fountains provided beauty as well as kept the water aerated.

Part of the Lawn Grove Farm of George Bergen became the eastside park, the last of the four large parks the Springfield Pleasure Driveway and Park District board determined to build. Named Bergen Park, part of the land had been in continuous ownership by the Bergen family since the First Presbyterian Church pastor, Rev. John G. Bergen, purchased an eighty-acre tract in 1830 from the federal government. Photo 1915.

The offerings of Krous Park were typical—benches, tables, winding walks, concession stand, a bandstand, dance pavilion, and an athletic field to accommodate the increased interest in physical activity by way of sports. Krous Park was, however, a private beer garden at Amos and Governor streets. Many neighbors in West Springfield did not approve and wanted it closed. Nonetheless, it prospered, and owner John C. Krous was proud enough to have a picture of it etched on his grave monument.

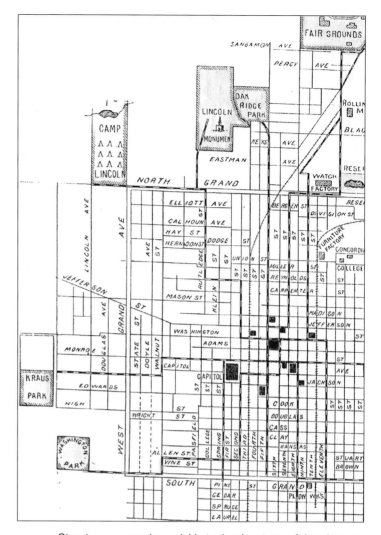

Streetcar companies quickly took advantage of the city residents' desire to get out into the country and developed parks at the edges of town. This 1898 map shows streetcar lines and three such parks—Oak Ridge, Washington, and Krous. The state fairgrounds and the city-owned Reservoir Park were also popular destinations.

Trolley parties were very popular at the turn of the century. Church groups, organizations, and even the streetcar companies themselves planned them. They were a profitable way to increase ridership on the weekends.

Amusement Parks

By the second half of the nineteenth century, urban residents had more leisure time and more disposable income than ever before. For amusement they turned to commercial entertainment. Amusement parks capitalized on this, drawing people out for thrill rides such as roller coasters, dazzling them with circus show, and entertaining them with concerts by popular bands and evenings of dancing. Springfield at the start of the 1900s had three such parks: Zoo, Mildred, and White City parks. All three were gone by the 1930s. The last one—Dreamland Park—opened in 1921 and reached its heyday in the 1930s and 1940s, offering dances and other entertainment especially Negro League Baseball games.

Zoo Park promoted itself as offering refined and educational entertainment. It took its name from the animals kept at the park: a camel, several buffalo, monkeys, and a small herd of deer. The large Arcade Building, pictured here, provided all the popcorn, peanuts, candy, soda, and sandwiches a park-goer would want.

The strolling walk to the dance pavilion remained an active part of the park after the rest closed down. A number of big-name bands played there.

Zoo Park was located on 150 acres on North Eighth Street Road and went east to the Sangamon River. Its "mammoth velvet roller coaster" was never used. When the park was built the owners were counting on a proposed extension of the interurban trolley to bring customers. That never happened. Later the buffalo were taken to the state fairgrounds after Zoo Park closed.

Mildred Park, named for the wife of Elijah Foster Iles, nephew of town founder Elijah Iles, was outside Springfield in a part of present-day Bunn Park. It featured a large lagoon with a shoot-the-chute for swimmers, picnic grounds and an amusement area with rides, a staging area for traveling acrobatic and death defying acts, and a dance pavilion. Park employees are shown in a photo of about 1915. Robert Cory is second from the left.

The mile-long, figure-eight roller coaster in Mildred Park provided thrills for many as did entertainment such as the electric fountain and the electric stage, which once displayed a scale replica of the San Francisco Earthquake.

When it opened in 1906, White City became a major competitor for other amusement parks. Located on East Capitol Avenue along the interurban line, it drew customers from both Springfield and Decatur and the small towns in between. Jaycee Park is located at the site today. White City overwhelmed the other parks with its rides, vaudeville acts, and big-name band entertainment. The park remained open into the 1930s, but its rides deteriorated and it became more of a picnic park than an amusement park.

Illinois State Fair

The first Illinois State Fair, organized by the newly-formed Illinois State Agricultural Society, was held in Springfield in 1853. For the next forty years it moved from city to city, until 1894 when it was permanently located here. From the 156-acres of 1894, the grounds grew to their present 366-acre size. The fair began as an education effort aimed at Illinois farmers who were, in the Society's words, "as a whole...necessarily among the most ignorant and bigoted members of the community, as they read little and travel less, so has been the more difficult to induce them to adopt improvements in their art."

A state fair was an inexpensive and popular remedy for farmer education. Traditionally held in September after farm work slowed, the dates were moved back to August in the 1920s as Illinois (and America) urbanized and the fair focused more on entertainment and selling of products. The first permanent building, the Exhibition Building of 1894, still stands, but sadly gone are the castle-like Machinery Hall, gargantuan Dome Building, Woman's Building, and dozens of historic barns and other structures. The grounds were named to the National Register of Historic Places in 1990. While still having an agricultural base, today's fair draws a wide audience interested in carnival amusements; concerts; auto, motorcycle and horse-racing, an ethnic village, and all manner of foods.

State fairs always provide an excellent opportunity for farmers to see the latest in farming equipment. This photo captures a Case dealer extolling the traction features of a Case steam engine as it climbs up an inclined ramp.

Not until 1907 was the carnival permitted inside the state fairgrounds. It was held on the city's public square instead. Many feared it would lower the fair's dignified moral tone. When the carnival did come on the grounds, vendors and rides were restricted to a small valley known by the name "Happy Hollow." This view of Happy Hollow visitors was made about 1932.

The colossal Dome Building once dominated the State Fair landscape, standing east across the street from the Exposition Building. Its majestic round dome was purchased by fair officials from the 1893 Chicago World's Fair. Famed architect William LeBaron Jenney designed the iron-frame glass dome, then claimed to be the second-largest in the world.

In Springfield the dome housed horticultural exhibits, an assembly room and, for a time the offices, of the Illinois National Guard. Just before the opening of the 1917 fair, it was destroyed by a fire of mysterious origin. Salvaged brick and iron were used to construct the nearby Conservation Building in 1918.

LEN SMALL PRES.   J.F. PRATHER TREAS   B.M. DAVISON SECY
KANKAKEE   WILLIAMSVILLE   SPRINGFIELD

ILLINOIS STATE FAIR
SPRINGFIELD
"GREATEST FAIR ON EARTH" SEPT 15 TO 23 INCLUSIVE
SPECIAL FEATURES ATTRACTIONS
$85.000. IN PREMIUMS
$25.000. IN SPEED
THE FAIR OF QUALITY

The Illinois State Fair was once held in September rather than August. Farmers had many of their crops harvested by then and were able to attend and exhibit at this important agricultural event. Len Small, listed on this 1916 advertisement, took a keen interest in the fair. He realized that as more people left rural areas and moved to cities, it would be necessary to change the emphasis of the fair from agriculture to entertainment. The carnival, which had once been banned from the grounds, was admitted in 1907 and, when Small became Illinois' governor in the 1920s, he managed to get the fair moved to August to coincide with city families' traditional vacations.

The Exposition Building, the fair's first permanent building after its 1894 establishment in Springfield, still dominates the grounds. Originally it was connected to the palatial Dome Building by a covered wooden walkway forming a ceremonial arch across the main drive. Gradual deterioration and changing fashion brought the arch's demolition in the 1920s.

The Woman's Building of 1903, was a place set apart for the "gentle sex" in the rough, male-dominated world of cattle-shows, horseracing, and farm-implement demonstrations. Prominent in this postcard view from about 1908 is the latest novelty, the automobile already edging its way onto the fairgrounds. This invention would hasten the end of the old agrarian society which had given birth to the Illinois State Fair.

This birds-eye-view photo of the fairgrounds is facing west from Peoria Road. The castle-like building at the bottom is Machinery Hall, demolished in 1973. Its long, covered, exhibit area burned a few years later. The Coliseum and Exposition Building are in the center and old race track at right. A new track and grandstand were built in 1927. At the top of the photo is the western section of the grounds, which was leased by the state and provided space for campers visiting the fair. The area west of Eighth Street was not purchased until the late 1920s.

In the 1930s the Fair's agricultural focus increasingly gave way to popular entertainment. Harness and auto racing were popular events. "Better Babies" contests, motorcycle races, stage shows, dance bands, fashion parades, and beer gardens became more prominent as the decade wore on. A large carnival, ethnic folk dancing, and bocce ball tournaments were introduced. By 1937 attendance registered at more than one million. These gentlemen, participating in the Rolle Bolle tournament in the 1940s, represented that growing separation from primarily agriculture to entertainment events at the fair.

At the State Fair cattle show there are always more judges in the crowd than on the stand. The cattle are expected to be well-behaved despite the crowds, noise, and general confusion. The ritual-like rite of animal-judging holds great drama for the gathered farmers. This photo taken inside the Coliseum dates from the 1930s.

Dairy-farming was once an influential force in Illinois agriculture. Dairy farm constituency lobbied for erection of the State Fair's Dairy Building in 1903. The white-painted brick structure, designed by the firm of Reeves and Baillie, is one of the most frequently-visited sites at the fair. All manner of dairy products are promoted and sold—milk, ice cream, sundaes, shakes, and cheese. It has also housed the Butter Cow exhibit, a sculpture of a cow molded from butter, for over sixty-five years. This attentive group of lady "soda jerks" from 1949 appear ready to fill orders for the crowds of fairgoers in the days before the effects of cholesterol were known.

Politicking has been as much a part of the Illinois State Fair as the awarding of blue ribbons. This lively scene from August 18, 1954, shows a dancing Illinois Senator Paul Douglas (1948-1966) taking a turn with an admiring female campaign supporter while an enthusiastic crowd looks on. The down-home charm of this scene captured a first-place award for the photo from the Associated Press.

A scene familiar to hundreds of thousands since the early 1900s is the litter-strewn main entrance to the fairgrounds. This view, from about 1912, shows the tents from the midway or "Happy Hollow" at the left, with the Exposition Building of 1894 beyond. One unfortunate loss is the giant dome building peeking out of the treetops at right, destroyed by fire in 1917.

The blue ribbon, a county-fair tradition from as early as the eighteenth century, had special meaning at the Illinois State Fair. Housewives from across the state, in grim competition, would strive to outdo one another in quilting, canned jams, blueberry pie, or here, the best iced cake. This photograph from 1950 captures a proud champion and her prize ribbon.

The Illinois State Fair was heavily influenced by the major fairs or "Exhibitions" of the nineteenth century, where new inventions and household products were exhibited. The average person seldom had a chance to see these new products on a regular basis. Springfield's Exhibition Building, shown here about 1915, mimicked the grand exhibition buildings of the worlds' fairs. Row upon row of items were displayed giving the effect of a grand department store. Here fairgoers could buy everything from new electric light fixtures and player pianos to Farris Furnace and Lewis Lye.

Hot Wheels, Fast Track

This mid-1950s aerial view looking northwest shows the Illinois State Fair in full swing. The streets are lined with concession stands and crowds. The infield of the main race track is full of automobiles. Grandstand audiences watch the harness racers warming up.

Famous early racing-car driver Barney Oldfield raced at the Illinois State Fair in 1905. He gained a reputation for stunt driving by racing against airplanes, among other tricks. Oldfield returned other times driving his well-known "Blitzen Ben." This old track was the scene of many racing accidents, including one in 1910, which took the life of local driver LaRue Vredenburgh.

Horse racing was well-established in Illinois by the 1890s and had been a major attraction at all of the state fairs of the nineteenth century. It was not surprising that a main feature of the permanent state fairgrounds was a dirt racing track (there had been at least one private track at Springfield before.) This first fair track was laid out in 1905 with these pagoda-roofed platforms for judges.

The present grandstand and track were used for more than auto and horse-racing events during state fairs. Exhibitions of circus acts and novelties such as this photo of a team of miniature horses taken about 1960, were typical daytime events for audiences in the "stand". Dirt for the track was brought from the horserace-loving state of Kentucky when the Grandstand was built in 1928. Evening Grandstand shows have ranged from Bob Hope and Dolly Parton to the Chicago Symphony and the Beach Boys.

A passion for horse-breeding and racing came to Illinois early, brought by the first settlers from Kentucky, Tennessee, and Virginia. Showing and racing horses has been a big part of entertainment from the first state fair in the 1850s. An especially noted race was in 1859, the year the fair was held in Freeport when, "Four females actuated by a desire to exhibit themselves to a gaping multitude entered the ring on horseback...strong-minded and full of pluck, put their horses upon their speed and gave an exhibition of themselves (one of them especially) such as is rarely seen in so public a place." Harness racing eventually became the most popular form of horse racing and the jockeys have remained almost entirely male to this day. This view from the 1950s show the intensity of the sport.

4-H events were always a time for rural young people to show off their skills with animals. The livestock parade was once a daily feature at the Illinois State Fair, as this photograph from the 1930s shows.

The Realm of Women

Ladies clubs were legion in late nineteenth- and early twentieth-century America. Springfield was no exception. They were a diversion for genteel ladies beyond homemaking duties, offering a chance for socializing, study, discussion, gossip, and camaraderie. These Springfield ladies of about 1900, gathered on the steps of the J.T. Capps residence at 837 South Fifth Street to have their pictures taken. The carefully studied pose has "caught" the women in earnest conversation. On the second step, particularly, the center woman gazes raptly at her companion. Most of the ladies probably lived nearby in this fashionable neighborhood and could have belonged to any number of Springfield ladies' clubs at the turn of the century—Woman's Club, Art-Study Club, Literary, Via Christi, or plainly named "Every Wednesday Club." The neighborhood on south Fifth and Sixth streets adjacent to the "Aristocracy Hill" district around the Governor's Mansion, was a prosperous one. Mrs. Capps' husband, a successful manufacturer, built this new house in the latest Queen Anne style in the 1870s. The ginger-breaded porch is embowered with date palms and vines.

Organized in March 1929, with the motto, "A More Beautiful Springfield," Springfield's Civic Garden Club has been a tireless promoter of gardening for beauty, exercise and, later, environmental awareness and healing. An unfair but common dismissal of the club as a group of ladies in white gloves with trivial concerns about gladiolus, is belied by club members contributions to Springfield's attractiveness. Senator James M. Graham, an early president, inaugurated a program by which thousands of trees were planted by generations of school children. Later programs included major beautification and anti-litter programs, a scent garden for the blind, and "Squanto plots" for those with no place to garden. Most important was club members—especially Dr. and Mrs. T.J. Knudson's—work in establishing Springfield's Lincoln Memorial Garden, designed by world-famous designer and naturalist Jens Jenson in the early 1930s. Shown in this Springfield garden during the 1960s are some of the club's staunchest supporters.

This unidentified group of Springfield women of the 1890s has gathered for a dinner party. They are perhaps members of one of the dozens of ladies clubs that flourished in the city. Each place setting has been artfully laid with the knives at a rakish angle on the plates and complemented with a loose, airy arrangement of carnations. The ladies' lapels are decorated with ribboned tags—possibly souvenirs of the event.

Children at Play

Switzer children pose at Washington Park's mineral springs about 1908. The park has been a draw to area children since it opened in 1900. The elder boy, at left, proudly wears his long pants, a sign of maturity. His younger brother at right still has knickers and long stockings.

Summer, boys, and watermelons, an image Mark Twain capitalized on in *Huckelberry Finn,* has long struck a chord with readers. Watermelon parties were once popular in Springfield, as this scene from about 1905 shows. Mrs. George Edward Day was a Springfield artist, photographer, and author of children's books. At her charming cottage at Fourth and Scarritt streets, she produced hundreds of photographs using her own and neighborhood children. "We hated it", recalled her daughter, Mrs. Leigh Day Smith, nearly eighty years later. "We'd rather have been playing." Here the Day children and neighborhood friends seem happy to cooperate--for the chance to enjoy the large, juicy melons.

Play in the backyard with neighborhood children makes up a big part of our nostalgic memories of childhood. At the turn of the century and before, many people had a backyard grape arbor useful for games of hide-and-seek or playing house or war. In this scene from 1907, children are carefully poised at "play". The little boy is riding his broom "horse", but more and more purchased toys like the tricycle and four-wheeled vehicle are making their way into the world of children at play. George Switzer, father of at least three of these children, was an avid amateur photographer and spent hours posing his family for photos. This one was taken in their backyard at 808 South MacArthur.

"Playing for Keeps" was serious business in backyards and on sidewalks in Springfield for generations. The loser in such a marble game could go home lighter by several aggies or sulphites. These Springfield boys in knickers and striped pants are in rapt attention as the game progresses. The perfect circle has been made with string in this photo of about 1900.

For older generations, clipping grass on a weekly basis was more work than relaxation. The younger ones found recreation in helping haul the grass away. In this photo, a youngster gives a hand in trimming the yard.

Daily trucks selling small cartons of milk to neighborhood children were popular in the early 1950s. They were followed by frozen-treat trucks in the late '50s. These later vehicles were outfitted with serving windows and took on the appearance of travelling soda fountains. The Wareham Dairy Company was headquartered in Taylorville and served Springfield neighborhoods as shown in the early 1950s scene.

Backyard Wonders

Picnicking in the backyard or city park was a popular pastime in turn-of-the-century Springfield. Despite the fact that these people were enjoying "relaxed" dining, they brought much of the formal indoors with them, from freshly-ironed linen cloths to Sunday clothes. The young gentleman on the right sports a bow tie and celluloid collar.

Members of an unidentified Springfield family relax in a swing made for a foursome on a quiet afternoon in the backyard. Notice the adjustable arms on the swing seats, predecessors of modern lawn furniture.

Gardening was a backyard activity that could be enjoyed by all ages. The pleasures of working with the soil and growing flowers and other plants is being imparted to these children participating in a Springfield Junior Garden Club program circa 1930. The children in front are holding some of the necessary "tools of the trade" and a selection of flower arrangements.

Picture-taking is an activity that has been enjoyed by many Springfield families over the generations. These young ladies enthusiastically pose for a fellow companion for this photo.

Miss Mary Ann Thoemmes (far left) sits with a group of ladies who appear to be preparing the backyard for a party in the vicinity of the 1100 block of South Twelfth Street. Tables have been made using boards and saw horses; a string of lanterns has been hung as well.

Members of the Noble B. Wiggins family enjoy the outdoors in this photo taken circa 1884 at the Leland farm, southwest of Springfield. The farm was used as a summer house for members of the Leland and Wiggins families. It also provided much of the food served to diners at Springfield's Leland Hotel, of which Wiggins was the proprietor. The Leland farm was later chopped into smaller parcels of land, which now make up parts of the villages of Leland Grove and Jerome.

Family reunions were often an enjoyable time for family members to get together and visit. This photo taken circa 1905 shows the large reunion of the Rosina Miller family at the home of her daughter, Mrs. Charles T. Bauman, 956 North First Street.

One of the best remembered social clubs of its time, the Capital City Cycling Club, organized in 1887, was comprised of many prominent Springfield citizens, both young and old. This photo shows a group of the club members at a picnic held at the Young brother's farm east of Springfield.

The Wentworth Club, once recognized as a powerful political group in Sangamon County, was first organized for both Republicans and Democrats. The club, which soon took on a political cast, was named for Dr. Charles Wentworth Compton.

Membership grew to over 3,000 before it was disbanded in the early 1930s. A group of club members enjoy a picnic at the clubhouse grounds northeast of Springfield in this 1902 photo.

Members of the Capital City Cycling Club posed for this picture in front of a bluff above the Sangamon River on the John and Joseph Young farm, located east of Springfield in Clearlake Township. The farm was a favorite site for weekly picnics held by the club. This photo was taken circa 1900.

Up in the Air

Governor Henry Horner and famous aviatrix Amelia Earhart were among those on hand for the dedication of Springfield's Municipal Airport on October 21, 1934. More than 15,000 people attended the opening ceremonies of the reconstructed airstrip, which replaced the old Commercial Airport operated by Craig Isbell and Gelder Lockwood. Shown here (left to right) are Governor Horner, Amelia Earhart, unidentified, Howard Knotts, and Elizabeth "Sissy" Knotts.

This scene at Municipal Airport's second annual "Springfield Day" was the climax of Aviation Week in Springfield. The weeklong event featured dinners, lectures and model airplane contests. "Springfield Day," which was held on the last day of that week, attracted thousands of visitors to the airport including Governor Horner. Over 50 civil and military aircraft were displayed and 300 passengers were taken on aerial tours of the city and Lake Springfield.

Springfield's Municipal Airport was the scene of many exciting air shows. One of the most spectacular was the "Reckless" Rex Murphy air and ground show which came to Springfield on June 12, 1938. The event, which drew 20,000 people, included such stunts as Murphy taking off in a plane on the top of a car and then landing on the car again. This photograph shows some of the show's airplanes flying over the airport.

This blimp leased by the Enna Jettick shoe company stopped in Springfield on November 11, 1931, as part of a goodwill and advertising tour promoted by the company. The air ship, the first in Springfield, attracted hundreds of people to Springfield's Commercial Airport. Arthur W. Luers, local Enna Jettick dealer, and his son, Arthur, Jr., were given an aerial tour of downtown Springfield before the blimp moved on to St. Louis.

Aviator Lincoln Beachy defeated driver William Endicott in a three-mile race held at the Illinois State Fairgrounds on September 27, 1914. "Earth vs. Air" racing contests became popular at the Illinois State Fair with the first race held in 1910 between renowned race car driver Barney Oldfield and pilot Archie Hoxsey. Hoxsey won the race. "Farmer Bill" Endicott was arrested weeks earlier for racing his car on one of Springfield's streets. Endicott is misidentified as Oldfield in this photo.

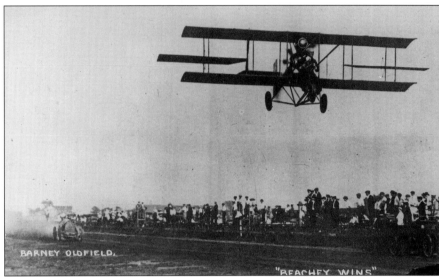

The dozens of cars parked along Route 4 and in the field next to Springfield's Southwest Airport attest to the popularity of many events held at the airfield during the late 1920's and 1930s. Large crowds of spectators often came to the field.

The children and grandchildren of Springfield's first settlers and self-made businessmen led a life filled with luxuries undreamed of a few generations earlier. Richly-appointed houses, elaborate clothes, and dinner parties were just a few of the ways Springfield's young, upper-middle class amused itself a century ago. Here members of that crowd pose for the camera imitating their more sophisticated elders in their idea of a smart dinner party. Note the chafing dish, a popular accessory for intimate dinner parties at the turn of the century. This Springfield scene is identified only as "Flashlight taken at Hay's [probably Charles Hay 821 South Second] August 12, 1896."

Commonly known as the "One Hundred Days Governor," John Stelle occupied the Illinois Governor's office upon the death of scholarly bachelor Henry Horner in 1940. Stelle immediately opened the Executive Mansion for a series of memorable parties, where liquor and entertainment seekers were in great supply. The cocktail party had become a firmly established Springfield tradition during prohibition, when illicit drinking parties in the home became a routine for many.

This unidentified Springfield interior of the early 1900s emphasizes the change in entertainment over the previous generation. Young people now held mixed-group parties and their behavior and manners were casual enough to shock the older generation. This relaxed group of merrymakers pauses to have its photograph taken. So advanced had photography become that amateurs with simple equipment could now shoot "flashlight" pictures indoors.

The phonograph or "Victrola" brought the world of entertainment into Springfield homes. Selections ranged from "high brow" recordings of Fritz Kreisler and Alma Gluck to the vaudeville antics of Gallagher and Shean, as well as ethnic and dialect songs. Here the four sons of Dr. Charles Patton are carefully posed around the family phonograph. The scene anticipates the coming of latter-day "entertainment centers."

Dressing up for a ride out in a stylish carriage—long a popular Springfield pastime—reached great heights the last week of September 1899. An elaborate "floral parade" of carriages was on procession to dedicate the new Woman's Building at the State Fairgrounds. Mrs. John C. Lanphier, chairperson of the event, recalled there were seventy-five "beautifully embellished carriages, phaetons, and other equipages" in the line. Over 250,000 live flowers were used in decoration. Mrs. Jerome Leland was enthroned on a chrysanthemum-decked "Queen's float." These three views show parade entrants the morning of the procession.

Flowers were gathered fresh or delivered from city florists early in the morning. This carriage sported large artificial flower wheelcovers— a savings of time and flowers.

The family pony, here ridden by a young man, was also garlanded for the procession.

Springfield has always turned out for a parade, no matter the occasion.

In this photo, taken May 11, 1898, during the Spanish-American War, the bugle corps of the Illinois Volunteer 5th Regiment marched down Fifth Street at Monroe. The troops were on their way to the Governor's Mansion to be reviewed by Governor John Tanner.

The 1931 rededication of the Lincoln Tomb brought President Herbert Hoover to Springfield and was a cause for great celebration. The Grand Army of the Republic was featured prominently as were automobiles full of dignitaries and state and local officials. The view is from Washington Street on the north side of the public square facing northwest.

An American Legion convention in September 1926, opened with a parade heading north on Sixth Street on the east side of the public square. Crowds line the street and watch from windows above.

Springfield's Municipal Band, and its segregated counterpart, the Colored Municipal Band, were crowd pleasers for generations of Springfield parade watchers. This circa 1940 scene is facing southwest at Fifth and Monroe streets. The sign for Diana Sweets Shop, is in the foreground. Claypool's soda fountain across the street was one of the most popular socializing spots in town for many years.

Increasingly, motorized "floats" became more important than marchers in city parades. While many were quite elaborate, others, such as this Cosmopolitan Club entry from the Christmas parade of about 1956, were startlingly simple. The Central Iron and Metal Company truck has been spray-painted with artificial snow to make up for a lack of the real thing. The south side of the public square is shown in the background.

Springfield turns out to admire a procession of Boy Scouts. The parade is heading north on Sixth Street at Jefferson. The building at center left is the old Chatterton Opera House. Motorists line the curb, standing by their autos for a better view of the parade.

Live reindeer pulling "Santa's Sleigh" were the main feature of this circa 1930 Christmas parade on the north side of the square.

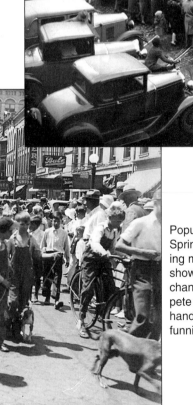

Popular amusements in 1930s Springfield were parades featuring man's best friend. These dog shows gave children and adults a chance to have their dogs compete in the largest, smallest, handsomest, best-behaved, and funniest categories.

"...In the summertime, there were plenty of circus parades," recalled Springfield resident George Bunn, Jr., about turn-of-the-century Springfield. "The more intrepid of us," said Bunn, would get a job carrying water for the animals' breakfasts and even have a place in the parade, which always came in the morning..." Many of the circuses visiting Springfield were down-at-the-heels, sad affairs where tired, ill-kept animals in small cages were paraded through city streets. These two photos of a circus procession are at Seventh and Miller streets around 1912. The lady and circus wagons in the center are from about 1920.

The Circus Comes to Town

Palaces of Pleasure

"Springfield has always been classed "as 'a good show' town," according to theater historian Henry House, writing in 1930. For a small pioneer community in the 1830s, Springfield had a varied and rich offering of amateur and professional theater. The dining room of Elijah Iles' luxurious new American House Hotel was outfitted for plays presented by the Isherwood and Mackenzie Company of Chicago. The company guaranteed to offer nothing "...that could pos-sibly offend the most fastidious delicacy." Certain religious factions worked constantly to end local theater productions (and most other enjoyable public entertainments). Feelings ran high on both sides of the issue. In 1839, the famous nineteenth-century actor Joseph Jefferson was so well received in Springfield that his company invested heavily in building a local theater. At completion, Jefferson recalled,

"... a heavy blow fell upon us. A religious revival

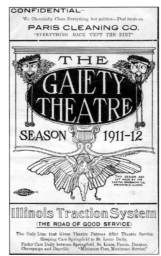

The inside of this Gaiety Theater program presented the current feature film—*Henry the VIII*—3,000 feet of handcolored film. A court scene with extravagant costumes, a hunting scene, and an elaborate banquet scene were to be a part of the film. This was one of the more elaborate of early silent films. The Gaiety, located at 509 East Monroe, served most often as a theatrical stage, and was the home of the local Gifford Players Stock Company. In 1929, the Gaiety became the Senate Theater.

By far the most high-toned theater in late nineteenth- and early twentieth-century Springfield was the Chatterton Opera House. Originally built by brewery-owner Robert Rudolph in 1866, it burned in 1876 and was rebuilt and later remodeled. Famous nineteenth-century actors and actresses performed here—Edwin Booth, Lotta Crabtree, Lillian Russell, Maurice Barrymore, and the D'Oyly Carte Players in Gilbert and Sullivan's *H.M.S. Pinafore*. Springfield jeweler George W. Chatterton purchased it as an amusement for his son. In addition to traveling professional companies, dozens of local amateurs (and Chatterton friends) got their chance to star. George Bunn, Jr.'s history of the theater mentioned a few—Hallie Elliott, Ada Richardson, Lulu Black, Gertrude Dement, Will Tracy, John W. Black, Jacob Bunn Jr., and Tom Kimber. The theater closed in 1924 and was replaced by the Orpheum Motion Picture Palace.

was in progress at the time, and the fathers of the church...by some political maneuver got the city to pass a new law enjoining a heavy license against our 'unholy' calling."

A young, newly-arrived attorney, Abraham Lincoln, was utterly disgusted by these pious shenanigans. He spoke before the city council "...with tact, skill, and humor, [keeping] the council in a roar of laughter...and the exorbitant tax was taken off." Lincoln took no fee for his work. Springfield entered its golden age of "legitimate" theatre in the mid-to-late nineteenth century.

The Metropolitan and Cook's halls opened in the 1850s and hosted performances by Springfield's first amateur theater group, the Thespians, in addition to traveling troupes. Burkhardt's Hall at Sixth and Washington streets opened in 1866 but was quickly eclipsed by Springfield's famous Chatterton Opera House. The Chatterton was opened by brewery-owner Robert Rudolph in 1866. After Rudolph's death and bankruptcy, jeweler George Chatterton purchased and renamed the opera house.

Nearly every famous actor and actress of the nineteenth century played the Chatterton as they traveled between St. Louis and Chicago. The Chatterton closed in 1924 and was replaced by the grand Orpheum Theater which featured motion pictures and live theater.

"The so-called 'Road' is no more; that is, there are few traveling companies," lamented Henry House in 1930. He believed that the need would be filled by local "little" theatre groups and stock companies. He was involved with Springfield's Community Players group, which was followed in the 1940s and '50s with Muni Opera and Theatre Guild organizations.

But to the majority of the public, theaters now meant movie houses. In addition to the gilded opulence of the 2,750 seat Orpheum, Springfield's audience could choose from films at the Tivoli, State, South Town, Pantheon, Roxy, Lincoln, Strand, and Esquire theaters. Today all of Springfield's downtown theaters have been demolished. While multiplexes offer numerous "screens" in mostly shopping center settings, the experience of dressing up and going out to the "movies" has been greatly diminished.

Mr. Frank Wiedlocher, owner of a wholesale and retail flour and feed business, owned the Central Music Hall building at Fourth and Jefferson streets in the 1890s. He rented out the second floor hall only to "the best patronizer." This circa 1898 photo shows the entrance to the hall. A tavern sits on the left and a grocery store on the right on the first floor with the flour and feed business entrance at the side.

"New and catchy scenery, which adds much to the interior" was mentioned in a 1900 description of Central Music Hall. One thousand twenty-five seats were available for concerts and theatrical performances. The spacious interior included a fine hardwood floor for dances.

The Empire's main-floor stage presented regular burlesque shows and reformers routinely criticized the place. At the "Stag Theater" upstairs, reported the Springfield Survey of 1918,—No sooner would a gentleman take his seat than "his box will be invaded by a young woman in short skirts who...invites herself to have a drink at the visitor's expense." While she "may be interrupted occasionally by the necessity of going on the stage, to participate in a bit of vocal or physical exercise, she will stay with her victim as long as her seductive companionship induces him to patronize the waiter."

The Kerasotes Empire

The first moving picture theaters, often call nickelodeons because of the nickel admission price, were once considered a passing fad by many. But Gus and Louis Kerasotes, two brothers who moved to Springfield from Chicago, saw in them an opportunity not to be ignored. They opened a nickelodeon, the Royal, in 1909. The silent films, which flickered images on a screen for six to ten minutes, improved rapidly and the Kerasotes Brothers expanded with the Savoy, Strand, and Senate theaters. The business expanded as a family venture when Gus's son George joined the firm. They also grew beyond Springfield. With a willingness to try new things—whether new sound systems or drive-in theaters—Kerasotes theaters flourished. Today a third generation of brothers and cousins remain very much involved with the operation of Kerasotes Theatres, a private business which weathered the Great Depression, the coming of television, and other changes which caused many theaters to close.

The Royal Theater opened in a storefront at 214 South Sixth Street, the first theater operated by Gus and Louis Kerasotes.

When the Strand Theater opened its doors in 1921, its theater organ, which produced the sound effects of horses' hooves, steamboat whistles, etc., to accompany the silent films, amazed moviegoers. After the "talkies" came along, the Strand was the first to install R.S.A. Photophone sound equipment, then considered to be the finest available.

The two brothers, Gus and Louis, founders of Kerasotes Brothers, are pictured in 1953 in the front row center. George G. is on the left and Nicolas is on the right in the front row. Back row left to right are Louis G., Stephen, Christine (Mrs. Nickas Yiannias), George L., and John.

The Majestic

When it opened at 419 South Fifth Street in 1907, the Majestic Theater sat between First Christian Church on the south and two residences on the north. The Majestic had high hopes of competing with the Chatterton as a prestigious legitimate theatre. It wasn't long, though, before it found itself a part of the RK0 (Radio Keith Orpheum) vaudeville circuit. When the Springfield movie theater entrepreneur, W.W. Watts, purchased the theater in 1914, motion pictures became part of the programs.

Jack Benny and Will Rogers were just two of the hundreds of vaudeville acts who performed on the Majestic stage. The stage had a forty-foot depth, large enough to handle a variety of elaborate productions and some less elaborate, but very popular, amateur nights. Local theater groups like the Gifford Stock Company also played at the Majestic.

The Frisina Amusement Company took over the old Majestic in 1935 and turned it into a first-run "photoplay house." (The film industry was still struggling with its own identity separate from theatrical performances). It was renamed the Roxy. Two major remodelings, (in 1935 and 1950) made the interior of the old Majestic unrecognizable. The stage was reduced in size so that audiences of up to 1500 people could be accommodated.

The theater building at 218 South Fifth Street began as W.W. Watts' Vaudette and directly across the street was the Harry T. Loper Lyric. The two theaters were among the most popular movie houses in town. In 1926 the Vaudette became the Lyric and under Loper's ownership had the claim of showing the city's first "talkie". It also boasted the first large screen and first Wurlitzer theater organ. In the days of silent movies, piano and organ accompaniment was an integral part of the show. The pianists kept their jobs for awhile after talking pictures were introduced, entertaining audiences during the changing of reels and as they entered and left the theater. (Photo circa 1926)

The Lyric became the Tivoli in 1929 when Frisina Amusement Company leased the building. The new Tivoli opened to "On with the Show,' Warner Bros. first 100 percent natural-color talking, singing, dancing, Vitaphone picture....One forgets entirely that it is a motion picture, or even a talking picture. The effect is utter reality," or so said the opening-day news article. This photo shows the Tivoli on the east side of Fifth Street looking south from Adams Street in 1937.

The marquee of the Fox Lincoln Theater at 329 South Fifth Street promoted its Vitaphone film circa 1930. But the theater's real fame came the day it hosted the world premiere for *Young Mr. Lincoln* in 1939. The hoopla created by the film's celebrities, executives, and newspapermen thrilled area residents. Lowell Thomas, the renowned radio announcer, was in Springfield to broadcast the events over the radio for those unable to get downtown. Marion Anderson, the "noted colored contralto," was on hand to sing a variety of selections during the pre-show ceremonies.

Lincoln Theater

Below: One of the last views of the Lincoln before it was demolished for a parking lot in 1976.

This special group of adults and kids, each with carnation boutonnieres, is read to enjoy one of the many family films in the 1940s. The Lincoln Theater is fondly remembered for its free Saturday morning shows for kids.

The Fox Lincoln, as it was called in this 1930s view, had its origins as the Princess Theater. The Unity Building constructed in 1884 served as home for the Y.M.C.A. and several businesses. After the "Y" moved, Tom Lawrence opened the Princess Theater in 1914 in the second-floor gymnasium. W.W. Watts later transformed part of the building into a "modern" theater. In 1929, 20th Century Fox purchased the theater, remodeled it further, and changed the name to the Fox Lincoln. When Fox sold it became just the Lincoln.

The Senate Theater marquee in 1934 celebrates the twenty-fifth anniversary of the Kerasotes Brothers motion-picture theater business. The theater itself, located at 509 East Monroe, was a bit older having opened in 1907 as the Gaiety. Kerasotes Brothers purchased it from retiring W.W. Watts in 1929 and changed the name to the Senate. The Senate was the last first-run theater in downtown Springfield. It closed in 1983.

The former First National Bank building on the southeast corner of Sixth and Washington streets was purchased by the Kerasotes Brothers and remodeled as the Strand Theater in 1921. At the left in this 1930s view is the Kerasotes Building, a three-story white terra-cotta structure on the northeast corner of Sixth and Washington streets, built in 1926.

Originally dubbed the Lincoln Square Theater, Springfield's Orpheum Theater rises to an eagerly-awaiting Springfield. The new million-dollar theater would replace Chatterton's Opera House, seen one block east at the far left in this 1926 photo.

The Elegant Orpheum

Gleaming white terra cotta exterior panels reflected the blaze of electric lights, giving the Orpheum a bright festive atmosphere. Theater-goers crowd the entrance on this Saturday night in 1930.

"$2 million Wonder Theater and Commercial Building," proclaimed the sign at the construction site of the future Orpheum Theater complex, even before it was officially named in 1927. Springfield truly received the gift of "a palace of rare beauty and elegance," in the new building at Fifth and Jefferson streets, said Mayor Emil Smith. The mayor lead the opening ceremonies which lasted an entire week. There were decorated streets, a Mardi Gras, parades, and flag ceremonies. For thirty-five cents anyone could step into the palace.

The complex provided a ballroom, cafe, eighteen stores, office rooms, a twelve-lane bowling alley and billiard rooms, as well as the spectacularly decorated theater. Built by the Great State Theaters, it was a major stop on the RKO vaudeville circuit, which brought to Springfield the biggest names in the entertainment business. The list is impressive—everyone from Al Jolson, Lena Horne, George Jessel, and Sophie Tucker, to Lawrence Welk, Duke Ellington, Desi Arnaz, Gene Krupa, and The Boston Pops Orchestra. First-run movies were also a part of the programs as was the fabulous Barton III organ, which rose up out of the orchestra pit for solo performances.

The palatial aura of the Orpheum Theater was created from the moment of approaching the intrically designed white terra-cotta structure. The interior decor was a rich baroque style featuring travertine marble floors in the entry, ivory and antique gold-plaster relief work on the walls and ceilings and mirrors, crystal chandeliers, and objects d'art on the mezzanine. Altogether, they created an escape to a world of entertainment not forgotten by anyone who attended a performance or program at the Orpheum.

A full house at the Orpheum was not at all unusual in the '30s, '40s, and '50s. The theater not only drew audiences for its regular programs, but also served as a civic auditorium for things such as the popular cooking classes sponsored by the *Illinois State Journal* and *Illinois State Register*. The audience shown is in attendance for a WCVS event about 1948.

The elaborately embellished plaster relief work can be seen above this signboard for the movie, *The Good Earth*.

Audiences entering on travertine marble floors had access to the mezzanine by way of the sweeping double staircase. The foyer ceiling was a full five stories up.

Antique reproduction furniture, glittering chandeliers with hundreds of prisms, and rich gold, red, and ivory colors of the mezzanine gave audiences a special place to converse during intermissions.

The Esquire, which opened in 1937, was one of the last of Springfield's neighborhood movie theaters to be built. Originally it was a second-run theater but was appointed with the latest equipment and even an adjacent parking lot, surfaced and lit. Many sought out the movie theaters during the hot summer months for their air-conditioned comfort.

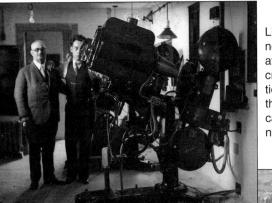

Life in the projection booth in the 1930s did not offer much time for watching the movie. Even after motorized projectors replaced the hand-cranked ones of the nickelodeon days the projectionist had a number of tasks to perform to keep the films running smoothly, including replacing the carbon in the projectors' arc lamps so they would not burn out during a showing.

World War II was over, cars were affordable, and there were many young families looking for an inexpensive night of entertainment. The drive-in movie theater filled that need. Snacks could be brought from home, the kids could be dressed in their pajamas are readied for bed, and there was no need to worry about disturbing strangers in the next seat as viewers stayed in their own cars. Young couples also found the unchaperoned privacy of the automobile irresistible. The Springfield Drive-In, pictured here, was built in 1947 with a 1,200 car capacity. It was located off Route 29 and Bypass 66 (Dirksen Parkway).

Voices of the Airwaves

Private radio stations sprang up across the country in the early 1920s. Many were owned by merchants who had products to sell. Radio enthusiast would sit up for hours with their headsets trying to pick up signals from as far away as possible. WBBZ was an early station operated by the Abraham Lincoln Hotel in 1925. It featured entertainers performing in the hotel's dining room. Harold L. Dewing brought to Springfield its first commercial station, WCBS, in 1926. The station, housed in the St. Nicholas Hotel, was limited in power and broadcast hours by federal license. In 1946 the station changed its call letters to WCVS to allow the Columbia Broadcasting System use of CBS and was given boosted power and unlimited broadcasting hours. As a second and competing station, WTAX, began broadcasting in 1930. Jay A. Johnson and his associates owned WTAX, which operated in the Abraham Lincoln Hotel. Just as the movies developed "stars" there were radio personalities, too. Local announcers such as Harry S. Bradford, for example, had the popular "Official Street Forum of the Air" program.

Two eighty-five-foot towers shown above the Abraham Lincoln Hotel belonged to WTAX, which formally operated in Springfield on December 4, 1930, using a temporary studio on the fourth floor.

When WCBS (WCVS) went on the air in 1926, Carlin Baker was its first announcer. He later joined WTAX as a founder and part owner.

This early 1930s scene in the Abraham Lincoln Hotel shows some early WTAX equipment. Notice the 'candlestick' telephone on the desk and the padded walls to keep out background sound.

After leaving the Abraham Lincoln Hotel and moving into the Reisch Building, WTAX added an FM station and built a new studio on Cook Street and By-Pass 66 (Dirksen Parkway) in 1948 under the new management of Oliver J. Keller, Sr.

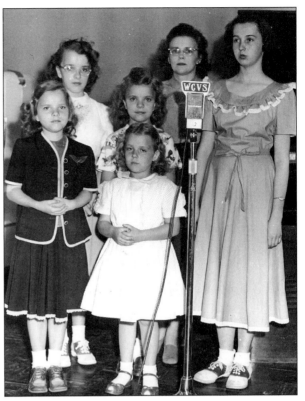

Organist and night-club entertainer Harry Wagner came to Springfield with the opening of the Lincoln Theater in 1928. The photo shows Wagner at the organ in the Majestic Theatre (Roxy) in 1933, from which WCBS (WCVS) broadcast a series of his organ concerts.

Early local radio programs sought out local talent such as the Junior Journal-Register singers, shown here in the 1940s when WCVS was located in the Leland Annex.

In 1928, Spizz Singer began his radio career on WCBS (WCVS). But he is most remembered for his work with WTAX beginning in 1938. His regular early morning farm show was on six days a week. Singer was responsible for many firsts in local radio and found time to be actively involved in the community. In 1962 a city street, Singer Avenue, was named in his honor.

Station WDAC at the Illinois Watch Company began broadcasting in the first days of radio. Many businesses used their own stations to advertise their products as well as to provide musical listening pleasure for local audiences.

Television

"Snow" had a new meaning for those Springfieldians who purchased television sets in the late 1940s and '50s. Static often interfered with the signals received from St. Louis, Rock Island and even Decatur. Then on September 30, 1953, a clear signal thrilled viewers with UHF (Ultra High Frequency) sets when WICS Channel 20 made its first program broadcast with the World Series game between the Yankees and Dodgers. Channel 20 sportscaster, Bernie Waterman did a pre-game show from the WICS studio at the Leland Hotel, the first local production. On the following Monday, October 1, regular scheduling began with local news, weather, sports, and programs such as "Captain Video" and "Dragnet," negotiated from network TV. Springfield TV sales boomed. Residents were as hooked as the rest of America on television. No other type of home entertainment has had as great an impact on the masses in so short a time. It was introduced at the 1939 World Fair and within ten years after World War II ended in 1945 it was a common item in the home.

Bill Wingerter (pictured above on the far right) began sponsoring a children's show to promote his Pegwill Packing Co. His Western Round-up and Pegwill Pete's Magic Circus ran ten years. A free hot dog, milk, and a chance to be on television kept children eager to participate. Wingerter went on to found WFMB radio and WRSP, Channel 55 television.

Announcer William R. Miller, playing Clicka T. Clack, hosted a late-afternoon children's program, The Funny Company. Occasionally the show offered local talent such as this young tap dancer.

Julie Craig was Channel 20's woman's editor for many years. Her locally produced, "The Julie Craig Show," was divided into two fifteen minute segments: "In the Kitchen" and "Shopping with Julie," featured every weekday afternoon in 1954.

Behind-the-scenes television made avid listeners of these teens shown here touring the WICS studio under the guidance of Helen Kinner in about 1958.

Promotion director, John Begue, gave weather without the aid of any 'high tech' computers, satellite pictures, or weather radar. Even the commercials were simply presented and commercial breaks were woven in as part of the program.

Channel 20's News Director Dale Coleman was THE voice for thousands of commercial and public-service announcements in the late 1950s and early 1960s. He is remembered by his coworkers as a tall, warm, outgoing farmboy from northern Illinois. At the time of his death at age 54 in 1983, he had become the Public Information Director at Springfield's Sangamon State University. This photo from about 1960 is how many remember him best.

On-site programming was difficult with cumbersome, heavy cameras requiring bright lights, as seen in this on-location shoot scene taken at the Lincoln Tomb.

A note on the back of the photo said:
"So weary-glad this droopy crew!
They lit the wick to put WICS 'thru,'
October 5th, in '53,
and brought in Springfield's first TV."

Milton Friedland (sixth from left) was WICS general manager for more than thirty years. Pictured here are most of the original staff of 1953: (L to R) Betty Mueller, Aggie Netznik, John Begue, Bernice Abner, Helen Kinner, Milt Friedland, Jim Harrelson, Jack Hoskins, Basil O'Hagen, and Dick Ashenfelter.

CHAPTER 4: SPRINGFIELD FORTISSIMO

The Springfield Civic Orchestra was organized in 1921 and performed until 1941, when it was disbanded for financial reasons. The Springfield Symphony Orchestra was incorporated in 1948 and was reorganized as the Illinois Symphony Orchestra in 1992. In the 1930s photo, conductor Wallace Grieves stands in front of the orchestra at the Knights of Columbus Hall. Grieves was conductor of the Civic Orchestra for its entire twenty-season history.

Histories of Springfield and Sangamon County are noticeably lacking in mention of the fine or performing arts. A "History of Art in Illinois" in 1904 despaired that "Art...has fought a long battle with two strong foes, the Puritan and the money-maker" and "during the last half-century the mammon-sewing drift of things has been even more powerful than the anathemas of a narrow pietism."

Despite this heritage, Springfield has supported a fair number of art clubs, music appreciation and performing groups, and theater, dance, and writing organizations. An aesthetic and literary education was always possible. Through such organizations as the Young Men's Lyceum of the 1830s or the Bettie Stuart Institute for young ladies, a conservatory of music. Classical music and an art study league were all prominent in nineteenth- and early twentieth-century Springfield. The oldest official arts organization in the city is the Springfield Art Association (1913), but dozens of groups centered on art, music, theater, poetry, and fiction have been available to Springfield citizens over the last century.

Strike up the Band

From military bands to orchestras to dance bands, Springfield has hosted a wide range of musical performers. One of the earliest bands, Butler's Band, was comprised of Civil War veterans and named for its leader, Edward Butler. Other popular bands of the nineteenth century included the Hibernian Band, the German Reed Band, and the Juvenile Band, which was made up of young males. B.F. Rogers, a black barber at the old Chenery House, formed the Rogers Cornet Band about 1870 with a dozen players. The Illinois Watch Factory Band, arguably one of Springfield's most famous, was formed in 1879 through the efforts of Jacob Bunn and Professor Louis Lehmann. Under Lehmann's direction, the band performed at many important events in Springfield. The band lost its affiliation with the factory in 1928 and formed the nucleus of the present municipal band, which was established in 1933.

Turn-of-the-century bands included the Court of

Formed in 1885, the Springfield Juvenile Band consisted of members ranging in ages from seventeen to twenty. The band changed its name to the 8th Illinois Regiment Band and later to the Fourth Illinois Regiment. Other band names included those of the Ide Engine Works and Sattley Manufacturing, each of which sponsored the band.

Many local bands had their own shows, which aired on Springfield's early radio stations. One such band, shown below, was led by Paul Termine and performed on station WCVS. Left to right are Norman Merrill, Paul Termine, Charles Peterson, and Louis W. Hahn.

Mandolin and guitar orchestras were in vogue countrywide at the turn of the century. Springfield had several high school mandolin and guitar clubs. One of the more unusual was Professor Blood's Ladies Orchestra, made up of several young women from St. Peter and Paul's Catholic Parish. Seated from left to right are Miss Maggie Maisenbacher, Miss Lucy Franz, Professer Fred W. Blood, Miss Nann Bernard, and Miss Marie Bernard. Standing left to right are Miss Louise Peter, Miss Minnie Nuess, and Miss Anna Nuess. This group lasted about three years and performed at church and other social gatherings.

Honor Band, the Greater Springfield Band, and the Cavalry Band. There have also been orchestras of varying size and abilities since Springfield's earliest days, but it wasn't until the formation of the Springfield Civic Orchestra in 1921 that Springfield had an orchestra of any longevity. The orchestra first performed in the old State Arsenal Building at Second and Monroe streets and moved later to the Knights of Columbus Hall at the southwest corner of Sixth and Edwards streets. Financial problems forced the dissolution of the orchestra in 1941. In 1948 the orchestra reorganized under the name of the Springfield Symphony Orchestra Association Incorporated. The orchestra is still going strong today as the Illinois Symphony Orchestra.

In the 1930s and '40s numerous dance bands were formed and performed in many of the clubs of Springfield. Some of the more notable were the Ray Cappella Band, George Rank and his Orchestra, the Kenney Barton Band and the Charlie Rodgers Band. Many of the bands stayed together for years and their leaders continued performing up to the time of their deaths.

One of Springfield's outstanding jazz musicians, Kenneth "Kenney" Barton, performed for nearly sixty years in local venues such as the old State House Inn, Sangamo Club, and the St. Nicholas, Leland and Abraham Lincoln hotels. Barton, a pianist, performed with his own orchestra, as a soloist, and as a member of the Fred Beck Quartet. The Kenney Barton Orchestra with Barton at the far right, is pictured here at the Masonic Hall in the late 1930s.

Trumpet player George Rank began his career performing with local groups like Del Courtney's band. By the 1950s Rank had his own orchestra, which was the Lake Club's "house band" for several years. This promotion shot of Rank was taken circa 1953. Rank would also become a local television celebrity in the late '50s and early '60s.

The Ray Capella Band, shown in this 1935 photo at the Abraham Lincoln Hotel's Club Lido, would later become the house band at The Mill Restaurant. Capella was known for smooth, soft music played for diners and dances.

Groups like the Charlie Rodgers Orchestra provided dancing music with the big band sound. The orchestra is pictured here at the Elks Club performing for the Lanphier High School alumni on Memorial Day, 1941.

Dances, receptions, banquets, or any occasion, Paul Termine's Band could provide the background music. An accomplished violinist, Termine played in a number of bands before directing his own group. This photo dates from the 1940s.

The Springfield Serenaders, a 1920s quintet, was comprised of a trumpet player, saxophonist, pianist, banjo picker, and drummer.

All the City's a Stage

The citizens of Springfield have been entertained by many amateur and professional theatrical groups as well as by national touring theater troupes. The earliest-known amateur theatrical group was the Springfield Thespian Society, which staged Springfield's first amateur theatrical performance, "The Charcoal Burner" in 1836. The Springfield Dramatic Club was another noteworthy nineteenth-century group whose members were made up of the sons and daughters of several prominent Springfield families. Many popular plays were performed by the Club at the Chatterton Opera House.

Organized in 1921, the Community Players of Springfield provided the city with active play productions for sixteen years under the direction of Henry House. House was also instrumental in forming another group—the Little Theatre Incorporated—in 1934. According to the group's incorporation papers, its object was to "create an interest in Drama; encourage the reading and presentation of plays, and other stage entertainments." The Little Theatre Inc., was a shortlived enterprise, disbanding in 1937.

The Springfield Theatre Guild and the Springfield Municipal Opera, both organized about mid-century, are still staging productions today. The Muni Opera, which can trace its roots back to a outdoor pageant written by William Dodd Chenery in 1935, was officially incorporated in 1950 and has presented plays at its Lake Springfield site to the present day. The Springfield Theatre Guild began in 1945, staging plays at various locations before erecting its own building at 101 East Lawrence in 1951.

Vaudeville actress Kathryn Kidd Eastman of Springfield poses in one of her lavishly decorated dresses about 1912.

This 1932 photo of the Community Player's production of "The Game of Chess" features Henry B. House (standing) as "Alexis Alexanderitich" and Frank J. Fischer as "Boris".

This scene from Act III of "Egypta" was performed in September 1908, at the Chatterton Opera House. The play was held to benefit the building fund of the Young Men's Christian Association. The words and music were written by Springfield native William Dodd Chenery. This self-proclaimed "extravaganza" featured over 100 actors with more than 300 children in the chorus.

A Springfield Players Company production in the 1920s features Henry House and Adelaide O'Brien (center).

Estill G. Gifford formed the Gifford Players stock company in 1925 at the old Majestic Theater. The company was comprised of four women and six men. Gifford's wife, Corrine, was the leading lady. The company moved in 1927 to the Gaiety Theater and left Springfield in 1931 but returned a few years later. This picture shows Gifford in the 1920s.

Ingenue Anna Nielsyn was a popular member of the Gifford Players. Here soft-focus camera work enhanced Miss Nielsen's self-consciously lady-like demeanor. Her softly-waved, bobbed hairdo, excrutiatingly-restrained outfit, and simple pearls contrast with a startling burst of feathers perched on her shoulder. The similarity of her name to a famous film star of the day, Anna Nilsson, could not help but make audiences remember it.

On November 6, 1951, the Springfield Theatre Guild staged *Born Yesterday,* the first play to be performed in its new facility at 101 East Lawrence. The auditorium could seat 482 and the lower lounge up to 200.

The cast of the Springfield Theatre Guild's production of Rogers and Hammerstein's *Flower Drum Song* poses for this 1965 news photograph. The cast explain that "living here is very much like Chop Suey."

Springfield's Municipal Opera, "The Muni," had its origin in a pageant by William Dodd Chenery as part of Lake Springfield's 1935 dedication ceremonies. Chenery envisioned an outdoor theater at the lake, an idea carried out by E. Carl Lundgren. A series of financial disasters, however, forced the fledgling enterprise to close by the mid-1950s. Fires in 1963 and '64 destroyed the site, but out of those ashes grew the Muni of today. This view shows the old stage in the 1950s being used for an Easter morning service.

Soft Shoes and Pas De Deux

Dancing has been an extremely popular Springfield pastime since the pre-Civil War "levees" and balls given during the winters when the General Assembly was in session. By the late nineteenth century, young gentlemen and ladies from polite society were expected to dance and belong to one of several dance clubs with names like "Our Awkward Dance Club," the "Qui Vives," "South Side Dancing Club," "Terpsichoreans," "Eronians," and the "Saltatorians." Hundreds learned to dance from Mr. and Mrs. Ira Fero beginning in the 1870s and from their daughter until 1935. Although routinely condemned by moralists as inherently wicked, dancing's popularity continued unchecked. Opportunities were available nightly—at society gatherings, large public halls, and in homes. A social survey of Springfield just before World War I noted that "to thousands of Springfield's young people dancing is a perfectly normal mode of social life." But, survey observers cautioned,

...the only feasible opportunity they have for enjoying it is now surrounded by moral pitfalls of the most dangerous and insidious in charac-

ter...public dance halls in Springfield where pass-out checks are given to the patrons which enable them to visit neighboring saloons...the young women in attendance may not only dance with partners who have been imbibing but, since introductions are not customarily required, [also with]...persons regarding whose irresponsible character and vicious habits they may be absolutely ignorant.

Springfield parents were warned that their children rushed to dance halls where "the fuses of licentiousness" are being lighted, and when "inevitable explosions take place, the citizens of Springfield will not be able to avoid a share of the responsibility."

The dancing craze of the 1920s fueled an ever greater appetite for dancing in Springfield—in night clubs, restaurants, private clubs, in masonic ballrooms, low-dives, and fashionable hotel ballrooms like the Leland and St. Nicholas—even the state fair. Dancing for all ages was a nearly universal pastime in Springfield until the early 1960s.

Lady members of the Saltatorian Dance Club in the late 1890s.

For many years ballet had a difficult time finding a permanent place in Springfield. Professional ballet dancer Mildred Caskey organized Springfield's Copper Coin Ballet Company in 1957—the first in central Illinois. Dorothy Proska Irvine followed in 1963 with the Ballet Concert Group. These eventually merged into today's Springfield Ballet Company, headed by Grace Luttrell Nanavati. Shown in this 1959 photo are a group of young dancers surrounding Dorothy Irvine and Mildred Caskey, seated in center.

Most recently the Springfield Ballet Company has been known for its annual performance of *The Nutcracker*. A 1960s production of *Cinderella* features aspiring Springfield dancers. Reel-to-reel tape recorders provide the background music.

Opportunities to dance were once everywhere in Springfield —nightclubs, restaurants, private clubs, and masonic halls, even the State Fair. But one of the most popular spots was the Leland Hotel Ballroom. This 1930 scene at the Leland shows employees of the Central Illinois Public Service (CIPS) Company and their sweethearts at a company dance. These company dances were a joy for many, but misery to the poor dancer.

The Abraham Lincoln Hotel was the scene of many high school proms like this one from 1959. Yards of chiffon and satin went into the making of a prom dress, which might never be worn again.

"Hops" were popular dances for teens in the 1950s and '60s. This one, held in the Leland Hotel Ballroom in about 1960, was broadcast on local television station WICS.

In 1913, Mrs. Alice Edwards Ferguson donated her parents' handsome Italianate Mansion to Springfield's Amateur Art Club as a city art gallery. The Edwards family was prominent in Springfield and Illinois history and had intermarried into Mary Lincoln's family. The Art Club eventually became the Springfield Art Association with an outstanding collection of American Indian and Asian art, a 3,000 volume library, 49 world-renown puppets, and American and European art. The house was restored in the late 1970s.

Society Belles and Balls

In 1930 the Springfield Art Association members inaugurated their "Beaux Arts Ball," Springfield's version of a debutante ball, with proceeds going toward maintenance of Edwards Place. Each year's ball is developed around a theme. This photo shows Miss Carylyn Becker, daughter of an insurance executive, exotically gowned for the 1952 "Pageant of the Peacocks" ball. "Magnificently arrayed" rhapsodized one reporter, "Miss Becker reigned over glowing maids...four special ladies in waiting and a host of fairies." While the ball is "a glamorous example of woman's continual ingenuity" said a news account twenty years later. It "...is not designed for snob-appeal."

The home of Alice Edwards Ferguson, who was responsible for the formation of the Springfield Art Association, on the grounds of Edwards Place. The handsome pressed-brick Queen Anne house was updated with a fresh coat of white paint and decked out in bunting in honor of President Theodore Roosevelt's 1903 visit to Springfield.

Choirs, Quartets, and Singing Societies

Springfield residents have always enjoyed public performances by choirs, band vocalists, visiting opera stars, and rock bands. But locals like to sing publicly as well. A German singing society was operating before the Civil War and numerous informal singing groups performed at public functions. A Springfield Philharmonic Society flourished in the 1860s and '70s and a second one formed about 1890. The latter "enlisted the best voices in Springfield and presented some memorable concerts," usually in Chatterton's Opera House. The "DeKoven Mandolin and Guitar Club" was a typical turn-of-the-century local amateur musical group.

Thomas C. Smith, son of a leading undertaker, was the club's principal soloist and "was in fine voice in those days," his favorite number being "the Elephant Song."

Others took their singing careers quite seriously, like Frederick Fisher, baritone soloist at Mary Todd Lincoln's funeral, or Mrs. E. Huntington Henkle, soprano soloist at the dedication of the Lincoln Tomb.

Some Springfield singers made a name for themselves far beyond Illinois, including County Sheriff Charles Arnold's daughter, Elinor, who became "a leading concert and orator or singer of New England." Then there was our own tenor Carlo Modino, remembered by Waldo Story Reed as returning to Springfield in the 1870s "with longish, wavy blond hair, carefully trimmed, blond mustache, and attired in a Prince Albert [coat], he was, indeed, a figure. Before he had gone away for a musical training he had been Charley Woods." Charley —"Carlo"—eventually became the grandfather of actor Robert Stack.

Springfield of a later era also produced "Skip Farrell, a crooner who recorded for Captiol records. Perhaps even better remembered was Tony Midiri, a cutter in Department forty-three at Sangamo Electric Company by day and at night a popular soloist for more than forty-six years. He debuted at the forerunner of the Lake Club in 1933 and last performed in March 1979, shortly before his death.

Springfield has had several singing groups including a barbershop chorus. But a group of Springfield women decided they wanted a chance in the limelight and so formed the female version of the barbershop choir on April 16, 1955, becoming the Sweet Adelines. The Adelines not only performed locally, but competed across the Midwest. As many as seventy women performed at one time.

The Springfield Municipal Choir was founded in 1938 from an idea by William Dodd Chenery. E. Carl Lundgren was its first director and remained in that position until his death in 1974. The choir, partially supported by the city, performs at no charge for local events. This photo shows the choir assembled on the stage of the Orpheum Theatre for an American Business Club fundraiser on June 27, 1947. Carl Lundgren is standing at the far left in the center group of men.

When Vandalia was Illinois' capital, legislators grumbled continuously about the poor quality of the food available. In Illinois, then called "the West", food for the public traveling by coach or horseback was often poor. One Easterner complained about a breakfast served to him during his travel in 1840s Illinois.

A meal so miscellaneous in character as to puzzle one to know whether it is intended for breakfast, dinner or supper—all sorts of pickles with a sweetened vinegar and stuff they call preserves...then peas and onions, peas and corn and radishes—Hot dough—light biscuit...Potatoes floating in a most unsightly liquid—with "Tea or coffee, Sir."

Humpert's 20th Century Lunch Room, 115 North Fifth Street. The lunchroom was an outgrowth of the original "free lunch" offered by saloon keepers to entice day customers. Springfield, like most towns, was full of saloons and many men were used to eating their mid-day (and evening) meals there. In Springfield's pioneer era, stagecoach stops and hotels had also always served food to the traveling public. Gradually, storefront businesses serving only food took over the saloon lunch tradition. Hundreds and hundreds of small restaurants have come and gone in Springfield. Humpert's capitalized on the modern sound of the new twentieth century in this circa 1908 photo.

"From such an amalgamation of substances," he told his wife, "you may suppose I made a glorious repast."

After wresting the capital from Vandalia, Springfield citizens knew they had to provide plentiful and tasty if not exotic food for the newly-arrived legislators. Thus began a long history of high-quality public dining for which Springfield eventually became noted. Elijah Iles' sumptuous American House Hotel was a popular gathering place and its public and private dining parlors were always in demand.

Springfield hotels and taverns (inns) provided not only food for the traveling public but for Springfield citizens as well. After the Civil War, the city's numerous saloons were providing a free lunch for customers to encourage their patronage. By the late 1870s, city directories advertised at least a dozen restaurants, mostly small, storefront places with a counter and stools where the working man could get a substantial meal. Prosperous businessmen, who did not return home for lunch, often ate at the large, fashionable public dining rooms of the Leland and St. Nicholas hotels.

It eventually became popular for ladies to meet for light luncheons in suitable public places. Several "confectioneries" and tea rooms catered to these women with light fare, including dainty sandwiches and sweets. Maldaner's Restaurant, with its popular olive-nut sandwiches, was one of these, maintaining its popularity as a luncheon spot for ladies well into the mid-twentieth century. But the mixed, or family restaurant became the standard before World War I. A 1912 guidebook to Springfield pictures several of these new, large restaurants such as "Springfield's most popular restaurant"

The Rollet Family Restaurant operated in several locations from the early 1900s until the 1930s. Their 613 East Capitol location is shown here about 1925. Note the use of white on uniforms, cloths, counter, even the stools. White showed dirt and spots easily and so had to be kept scrupulously clean and to give a sanitary appearance.

the "Angel Restaurant" at 517 East Monroe. Gone was the dominating counter, replaced by a larger room and numerous tables and chairs with starched white cloths.

The phenomenal growth of women in the working world in the 1920s—as secretaries, telephone operators, cashiers, receptionists and clerks,—meant many more lunching women customers. The downtown luncheonette, with its sparkling white counters and thrifty prices, sprouted by the dozens and appealed to these working women.

A newly mobile America (and Springfield) began to look for entertainment outside of the home. "Drive in" fast service restaurants became increasingly popular. To be able to drive up, get a quick meal—perhaps even have someone bring it to your car—was irresistible. One of Springfield's earliest—the Maid-rite—still operates. And of course, the heyday of drive-ins, the 1950s and '60s—found Springfield filled with franchises and locally-owned drive-ins with their ubiquitous "car hops". At the same time, others wanted "fine dining" with a night-club or elegant atmosphere and dancing to live music. Fishers Inn, an old farmhouse on West Jefferson that opened in the early 1930s, was the prototype for the suburban dining spot. Others followed: The Orchid Lounge, the Southern Aire, the Supper Club, Black Angus, The Cliffs, The Mill, Stevie's Latin Village, and the premier dining and entertainment mecca, the Lake Club.

Norman's Coffee Shop at 617 East Adams Street opened June 22, 1931, and was a popular spot for breakfast and lunch until 1966. The first manager was Mrs. Albert Triebel, who had a BS degree in Dietetics from the University of Illinois. Mrs Triebel supervised the making of a special coffee blend for the restaurant. During the hot summer months, the shop had another attraction—a twelve-ton air conditioner.

Jack O'Neil operated one of the hundreds of neighborhood restaurants that have existed in Springfield. In the days before most families owned an automobile, workers walked to nearby eateries like this for lunch. O'Neil's, at 1401 South Eleventh Street, catered to miners and factory workers from the Sattley/Hummer plant. O'Neil (center) stands with some of his customers in this 1912 photo.

Many Springfield restaurants were far from fancy but had many customers due to their good food and reasonable prices. The appropriately-named "Shack" Restaurant at Second and Jefferson streets was one such spot. Shown here during the 1940s, the menu proclaims that two eggs could be had for fifteen cents—"any style."

Theodore Gray, a Greek immigrant, once part owner of the Sugar Bowl Restaurant, opened his own restaurant at 1400 South Eighth Street about 1935. Known officially as "Grays," it was referred to affectionately as "Teddy Gray's" by hundreds of regular customers before it closed about 1956. This scene from about 1955 shows the building at Eighth and South Grand, which is still standing.

George & Sarah David opened Rose's Eat Shop lunchroom at Eighth and Monroe streets in downtown Springfield in the mid-1930s. However, at the end of World War II, the David's moved the business to 1107 East Ash for larger quarters and, what became increasingly important—more parking and less traffic congestion. The restaurant was a popular neighborhood gathering spot that even sponsored its own baseball team. The turn-of-the-century building with metal ceiling has been updated with Art-Deco-styled lights, chromium chairs and tables, and masonite-paneled bar.

When Route 66 was in its heyday in the 1950s, Stevi's Latin Village at 620 North Ninth Street was a popular tourist stop. Owner Steve Crifasi posted signs advertising the restaurant "from Chicago to St. Louis," according to former waitress Mae McMillen.

Illinois elected officials and governors were regulars and enjoyed the live entertainment. But, recalled Mae McMillen in 1993, "...the staff all had to be ready to do a song when our names were called." It was like amateur night there every night. Owner Steve Crifasi, shown standing, was not excepted. When called he often sang his favorite, "Brother, Can You Spare a Dime?"

The Cliffs
Routes 4, 36, and 54 West
Springfield, Illinois

In the 1940s Wabash Avenue was a narrow, two-lane "hard road," the main entrance to Springfield from the southwest. Houses and some businesses lined the street with more than a few cornfields interspersed. Moonlight Gardens (at Wabash and Chatham) brought entertainment seekers and several restaurants, such as The Cliffs, with large parking lots. A 1950 postcard advertised the restaurant as "originators of the famous salad bar." Today the Barrel Head Restaurant occupies this site.

Springfield restaurants increasingly followed the automobile to the outskirts of town, where land for parking lots was comparatively inexpensive. The Fleetwood Restaurant opened in 1957 on Business Route 66 and catered primarily to long-distance truck drivers. By the 1970s the restaurant had grown so popular that it remained open twenty-four-hours a day and served as many as 3,500 customers on a weekend. Illinois' Governor Jim Edgar was a great fan of the Fleetwood's deep-fat fried chicken until "treatment for a clogged artery" forced him to give it up in 1992. The next year the restaurant closed, a victim, according to owner John Howard, of franchise restaurants which made it "harder and harder to compete for the food dollar."

The Georgian Restaurant at Ninth Street and South Grand Avenue was a familiar landmark for years until it closed in 1986. The name was a play on the Georgian-revival style popularly interpreted in so much roadside architecture from New England to California during the 1920s through the 1950s. Open twenty-four-hours a day, breakfast was almost always available for those who kept non-traditional hours, and Georgian pies were famous throughout the city.

From 1927 to 1959 the Sugar Bowl at 900 South Grand Avenue West was one of Springfield's most popular restaurants. Greek immigrant owner Alekos Karahouzites' (shortened to Alec Karon) warm, friendly personality kept the public coming back. Homemade ice cream was available until the restaurant closed. Here the neatly-attired staff is shown with Karon far right. "Our motto...cleanliness," proclaimed the menu covers.

Uptown Eateries

The Markee Grill on the northeast corner of Seventh and Adams streets sports a new streamlined chromium front with plate-glass windows in this view from about 1947. Short-order food was served from the kitchen behind the counter.

Frank and Joe Saputo opened their restaurant at Eighth and Monroe streets in 1948, which still features family recipes from southern Italy. The "Twins Corner," as Saputo's was called, was one of the first spots in town to serve pizza. Still operating today, the restaurant has been remodeled several times since this 1956 photo was taken.

Brothers Paul and John Graham established a cigar store in 1901 on Monroe Street between Sixth and Seventh streets. A "sports department" kept customers informed about the scores in area and national sporting events. Gradually the store added more food items, becoming a full-service restaurant in the 1920s. Graham's grew so popular that the owners needed more space and moved to 221 South Sixth Street in 1936. This picture shows the restaurant as it appeared in 1958. The restaurant closed in 1965.

A funeral home, speakeasy, and finally tavern, Norb Andy's opened in the early 1930s. It has always been a popular gathering spot for the statehouse crowd. The business was named for former owner, Norbert Anderson. Former governors William Stratton, Henry Horner, Otto Kerner, and James Thompson were frequent diners here. The famous sailboat sign on Capitol Avenue once prepared customers for the nautical-theme interior. Norb's occupies the basement of the historic Hickox House at 518 East Capitol.

Ernesto Bensi, owned the Monarch Brewing Company distributorship and lived on the third floor of a building in the 100 block of North Sixth Street during prohibition. Some have said the Italian businessman dealt in bootleg liquor. Whatever the case, he opened the Monarch Tavern soon after repeal. The name was changed to Monarch Grill in 1941 when the building was fully modernized in the commercial Art-Deco/Streamline design with characteristic neon signs. It was "also a favorite spot for those seeking dancing and expertly mixed drinks. Music is furnished nightly by Nick Nicholas, direct from New York City on the Electric Hammond Organ," according to a 1940 advertisement.

Maldaner's is Springfield's oldest, continuously-operating restaurant. Founded as a confectionery and catering business in 1884, it grew to a tearoom and, finally, a full restaurant. A Maldaner's specialty was lemon cream sherbet made from Mary Todd Lincoln's personal recipe, which legend says was served at the Lincoln wedding. Isobel Smith, who began waiting tables at Maldaner's in 1938, remembered that all the pastries were made by an "old German baker" and waitress uniforms were "...a pretty maroon, a real dark maroon that went so well with the mahogany; and they had white, frilly aprons...." When the restaurant was fully renovated in 1977, the mahogany-toned wall panels were retained and old murals uncovered.

Cozy Dogs and Bowls of "Chilli"

Like every other aspect of American life, restaurants were dramatically affected by the rise of the automobile. Entire restaurants centered around the development of the car culture. Their main characteristics were fast service and large (usually electric) signs that could be seen easily by drivers. Three of Springfield's fast-food restaurants are shown here. The Cozy Drive Inn's original 1950s building on South Sixth was only recently demolished. Steak 'n Shake at Seventh Street and South Grand Avenue has been replaced by a newer fast food drive-in, but the Maid-Rite, Springfield's oldest drive-in (from the 1920s) remains in its original building and location at 118 North Pasfield.

Steak 'n Shake drive-in at Seventh and South Grand opened in 1950. One waitress, Faye Rankins, "hopped" cars from 1952 until the late 1980s. The restaurant was closed in 1988 and was demolished shortly after.

The Maid-rite Sandwich Shop, Pasfield and Jefferson streets, Springfield's oldest "drive-in" was named to the National Register of Historic Places in 1984.

The two top views are perfect social documents showing the effects of the automobile. People with cars moved further from the center of town and handsome old residential districts fell into commercial use. In the late '50s the Just-Rite Hamburger restaurant at 1531 East Cook occupies the front of an old house, as does the Dew Chilli Park Parlor below at 720 South Fifth Street.

Joe Bockelmann is credited with starting the Springfield tradition of putting two "Ls" in chilli in 1909. He consulted a dictionary at Lincoln Library. "Man! oh: Man! did that upset the sign painters around town," Bockelman recalled in 1969.

Jack Robinson moved to Springfield during the Great Depression and opened a diner in 1934. He dreamed of owning a whole chain of restaurants. He eventually had three. Restaurant historian Keith Sculle reports that Robinson developed these pre-fab, streamline-style white cubes of gleaming black and white porcelain. Unfortunately, this building at 512 South Grand Avenue East was completely covered over by a recent owner.

Top's Big Boy restaurants were an example of the giant fast-food franchises of the late 1950s and mid-1960s that came to Springfield. The oversize "big boy" was a popular feature of the restaurant, which was located at Fifth Street and South Grand Avenue until the 1980s.

"Walk on the Wild Side"

From its earliest days, Springfield had a reputation as a "wide open" town. In the 1850s, according to historian Paul Angle, there were at least twenty gambling houses in Springfield, "some of which were fitted up as elaborately as the glittering establishments of St. Louis and New Orleans...houses of ill fame were numerous." Wondered one contemporary, "Why were keepers of these places protected when the order-loving part of the community undertakes to rid their vicinity of these evils?" Apparently no answer was forthcoming, for a William Lloyd Clark, evangelistic minister of 1910 reported that:

"Northeast from the corner of Sixth and

Washington streets for many blocks the city of Springfield is a mass of dive saloons, pawn shops, questionable hotels, fourth-rate lodging houses and assignation resorts, stenchful restaurants and brothels from the lowest ramshackle hovels to the most elaborately equipped which can be found anywhere in the State."

City politicians and business leaders had come to favor the concept of segregating vice into its special district. Illinois Senate hearings about Springfield's notorious vice activities refered to this area as the "Tenderloin District" or "Levee." Concentrated in the area around Eighth and Washington streets, the Levee

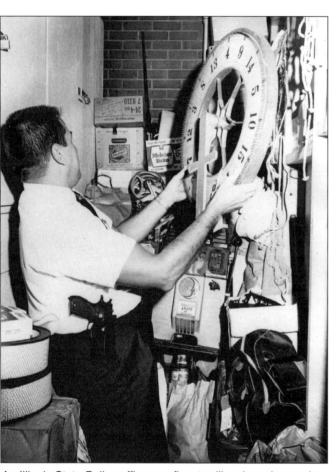

An Illinois State Police officer confiscates illegal gaming equipment in the 1950s. Mayor Nelson Howarth, Judge George Coutrakon, and attorney Charles Northrup were leading figures working to close down Springfield's notorious, widespread gambling in the early 1950s.

Verses and drawings by Jack Proctor, 1942.

Mrs. Matter
This Sodom, This Vanity Fair
This Washington street,
which pollutes the air
of our fair city
must be purged,

We must erase
its very name
if we hope to abolish sin;
There is where our efforts
must end and begin

That's what George,
my "husband",
always said—
Pour me a drink, Sam,
and let's go to bed.

Eddie
Washington Street
is where I meet
a man I can fight,
or spend the night
in a dive.

She's alive—
Old Washington Street—
with men I can beat
up when I'm drunk.

Minister William Lloyd Clark venemously described "the old Jezebel" Helen Payne and her "palatial brothel" at Eighth and Washington streets. The wages of sin must have paid pretty well. In the 1909 city directory, Payne has three telephone lines listed.

Payne Gregory J, bds 2007 n 9th
Payne Harry L, agt, rms Lafayette Hotel
PAYNE HELEN O MISS, Residence 121-123 N 8th, Tels B
1995, Inter-State 1851, Annex 2939
Payne John W, driver Grand Union Tea Co, res 2007 n 9th
Payne Lawrence (c), bds 1514 e Mason

was known throughout the central Midwest for its vice, drugs, gambling, and corruption. The profitable enterprises operated under the nose (and full awareness of) city officers. The "swell politician, tony young sport, or the prosperous looking businessman...pulled the political wire...while the ward heeler and party boss bumps elbows with the bums down in the dives to deliver votes," claimed Reverend Clark. He observed an auto filled with "fashionably dressed" men and women out in the public street laughing and who "...shamelessly quaffed the beverages of Hell. And down through the red light district the 'Red Devil' carried its load of rich and dissipated merrymakers, stopping and ordering drinks from the lowest shambles. Some day, before a just God, these stewards of wealth must render an account. But do they think of this?" fumed Clark.

Springfield's Levee was such an institution that Springfield artist Jack Proctor issued a small private book peopled with Levee characters and their stories in verse in the late 1930s or early '40s. Some of these are reproduced here. In the 1960s and '70s, the last vestiges of the old district were demolished in a major urban renewal sweep.

About that time a popular local joke making the rounds concerned the new Horace Mann Insurance building on the site of Helen Payne's famous brothel. A former resident, having been away for many years returned to see the gleaming new structure and remarked that the old Madame had certainly done well for herself.

The raucous entertainment shown here took place in front of the Jefferson House at Seventh and Washington streets. "The Power of Music," as the satirical painting was called, was created in 1885 by John Mahony, Wabash Railroad laborer, occasional artist, and regular Jefferson House customer. The saloon/hotel operated from the mid-1800s until about 1910. Stories from old timers say that the place was a popular gathering spot for city aldermen after council meetings.

Dopey
There are three kinds of people:
High brow, low brow, and no brow,
and I am the last.

I don't know how
I got here,
I don't remember
the year...

I don't recall
And here,
I live,
sensing, never thinking,...

Eating and sleeping and drinking,
spending weekends caught
in the narcotic joy of being.

Looking more pathetic than wicked, this early-morning view shows the heart of Springfield's Levee at Eighth and Washington streets about 1918. By night darkness covered the aging buildings and electric lights glowed from the bars which lined the streets. "Vile and stenchful, including ...Negro-dive saloons. Bohemian saloons where the English language is never spoken. Blazing lighthouses of Hell and recruiting stations for the penitentiary," fulminated temperance minister William Lloyd Clark.

Hot Spots

Illicit drinking in "speakeasies" during the 1920s gave way to legitimate "nightclubbing" in the 1930s and '40s. But the excitement of an evening out was still important for attracting business. Springfield restaurants often provided places for dancing to live music. And, like movie theaters, many night spots began to decorate in the escapist manner, which helped people forget the work-a-day world. At the high end were smart clubs like the Lake Club with a railing-surrounded raised dance floor and moderne-inspired curved walls. Then there was the Blue Danube Nightclub's novel lighted "Wonder-Bar." Other night spots like Fisher's Inn and the SoHo swathed their walls in miles of satin-like material. Sadly, that material was prone to catching fire, as SoHo owners found out when the club went up in a spectacular blaze in 1940. The swankest places, it seems, used "club" or "lounge" in their name and styled themselves on anything New Yorkish.

The Lake Club
Springfield, Illinois

The Villa Valencia, Peacock Inn, and even an ice-skating rink known as the Joy Inn, all came and went in this building before it began its almost magical life as the Lake Club about 1940. Dance promoters Harold Henderson and Hugo Giovagnoli redecorated the building and concentrated on providing Springfield with big-name entertainment. Nelson Eddy, Spike Jones, the Inkspots, and Ted Lewis performing there, as did Jan Garber, Woody Herman, Russ Morgan, Henry Bussee and Tiny Hill. Entertainers and big bands brought capacity crowds to this room week after week. By 1970 the club was closed and shuttered, a victim of changing entertainment fashion.

After a few unsuccessful attempts to re-open the Lake Club—including a stint as "The Sober Duck Disco", the old Lake Club building on Fox Bridge Road ended with a fire in September 1992. Photo courtesy of *State Journal-Register*.

Joseph Maero, proprietor of the old Ken Hotel at Ninth and Jefferson streets, opened his own bar in 1933 at the end of prohibition. He chose a building on the southwest corner of Fourth and Jefferson streets across from the St. Nicholas Hotel, and decorated it in smart, white modern furnishings. Drinks served at small tables with piano-playing and singing provided an intimate setting. The SoHo was a popular night spot and, after a fire, was enlarged into a full restaurant—this time with less-fire-prone knotty-pine panelling. Later, in an attempt to attract new customers, son Felix opened the Oriental "Ho-Toi" room and Chez' Felix private club. The SoHo closed in 1965.

Scintillating beauty and relaxing atmosphere," said one ad for The Last Word Lounge in the early 1950s. "It should be on everyones must list." The bar, located at 411 East Washington Street, was operated by Celso Rubini. It opened about 1950 and closed ten years later. Advertisements stressed the modernity and novelty in its decor.

THE LAST WORD
"ESSENCE OF BEAUTY"
411 E. Washington St.
Springfield, Illinois

Cansler's Lounge at 807 East Washington was opened by Leslie Cansler about 1948. It was a well-known place where jazz musicians playing in Springfield went after their gigs were finished. Cansler later moved the lounge to 423 East Washington Street about 1966. Cansler died a year later.

Fisher's Inn

In 1927, Mr. and Mrs. Glen converted their fifty-year-old farm house into a restaurant specializing in chicken dinners. The house, located near present-day Jefferson Street and Churchill Drive, was then about three miles outside of town. It became a popular dining spot, The pleasant, rural setting played a part in advertising—"the big sweep of lawn, with century old trees," and land which "...rolls away in a deep ravine" gave "a grand view and does add to the enjoyment of the dinner." The restaurant's name later changed to "The Farm." It burned in 1951.

Diners were seated in this large tented space with the support column mocked up as a palm tree. A bandstand at right provided music for dancing and the bar on the left promised that: "anything in mixed drinks can be secured. In fact, the man who serves you would like to hear of a drink he cannot make."

The old farmhouse entrance hall with columns and angles, highly-varnished mantel and stairs, was barely visible beneath a concoction of fabric which draped everything in sight. This Arabian tent fantasy is brought down to earth by the Grand Rapids furniture (circa 1910) and an iron radiator.

One in a Mill-ion

The Mill owners Herman Cohen (left) and his nephew Richard Cohen (right) in the 1950s.

Springfield's Mill Restaurant, at Fifteenth and Matheny streets, had a reputation throughout central Illinois for fine food and entertainment. Around 1918, brothers Louis and Herman Cohen opened a grocery store on the site. Following a major fire, the store reopened as a restaurant in the early 1930s. Louis' son, Richard, joined as a partner in 1946. The original restaurant, shown above in about 1932, was spartan by later standards—wood floors, bentwood chairs, heavy wood tables and booths, and large ceiling fans hanging from the old tin grocery store ceiling.

Good food and service brought in customers and the building was remodeled and redecorated several times. Seating capacity went from 40 to 500 by the time the luxurious curves of its modern Baroque decor were in place in this 1963 view. Governors, politicians, and even Hollywood stars playing the State Fair dined here. Local bands, including Ray Capella, entertained nightly. The cigar-smoking Herman and his nephew Richard (above left) treated guests with special attention. The Cohens sold the business in 1971. The next year the building was destroyed by fire.

Watering Holes

Taverns in the United States developed from the male-dominated saloon of the nineteenth and early twentieth century to the neighborhood bar of the mid-twentieth century, where both men and women gathered after work to socialize. Several of these neighborhood bars still exist in Springfield today, strong survivors amidst the current crop of cocktail lounges and "upscale" bars patronized by young professionals. The neighborhood bar usually offered spartan decor consisting of wooden or chrome stools, tables and chairs, a grill for short-order foods and, later, racks for holding chips, beer nuts, and other snacks. Draft beer by the glass or a jug filled to take home was the main offering. Socializing was and remains the primary entertainment attraction.

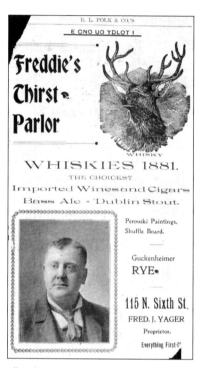

Freddie's Thirst Parlor at 115 North Sixth Street was owned by Fred Yager, and typical of the hundreds of saloons that once operated in Springfield. The saloon was a place for cigar-smoking, tobacco chewing (and spitting), and whisky-drinking. The Old Elk Whisky Company has a special promotion in this photo from about 1895. Sign on the curb offers "Bass ales, Dublin stout, Old Tom gin, and Mum's and White champagne along with shuffleboard."

While nearly all saloons were listed in the city directory, and some even advertised, few did so with Fred Yager's flourish. Elk's 1881 Whisky is his offering of choice—its logo getting almost as much space as the photo of a neatly-tailored Freddie shown here in this 1898 city directory ad.

The Illini Bar at the northeast corner of First and Jefferson streets was typical of the dozens of corner taverns throughout the city at the turn of the century. At left, Reisch Brewery wagons deliver fresh kegs of beer in this circa 1912 photo.

Fred Noll ran a workingman's saloon at Thirteenth and Reservoir streets in the early 1900s. Workers from the old Illinois Watch Factory and International Shoe Factory and other area employers made Noll's a popular gathering spot. These gentlemen pose with their mugs of dark beer outside Noll's in about 1913. The bartender, Frank Lucas, is in the front row, second from the left. Noll, according to one newspaper account, sold from "eight to ten half barrels a day." The building was later a grocery store.

An unidentified Springfield bar during World War II. Many Springfield taverns were still predominantly male in the 1940s and '50s. This after-work crowd (the clock says 4:32) enjoys bottled beer. Signs advertise everything from Pearl Beer and Coca Cola to Raleigh Cigarettes and "American Labor...producing for attack." Typical are the ice coolers and sinks behind the bar and ceiling fans overhead.

Until it closed after a fire in 1992, the Argonne was Springfield's longest-operating bar. John Mezo opened the Argonne in 1933, immediately upon repeal of Prohibition. The bar operated at 407 East Jefferson Street until the 1980s when it moved to North Fifth Street, then East Washington Street. The row of bars along Jefferson Street offered drinks and entertainment, including some female dancers whose artistry precipitated police raids on a regular basis in the 1950s and '60s.

Eddie Eck worked at the Par-A-Dice sandwich shop at 1710 South MacArthur Avenue in the early 1930s. Shortly after Prohibition ended he opened a small bar down the street at 2001 South MacArthur (then West Grand) Avenue. Called the Grand Inn, the place became a popular neighborhood congregating spot for families. This photo from 1963 was taken shortly before the Grand Inn closed.

Springfield tailor Peter Troesch went into the grocery and saloon business about 1906 at 231 West Mason Street. According to family descendants, Troesch used money earned from the saloon to keep the grocery going because it had several customers who had been extended credit. Unfortunately, he was forced to close the saloon during Prohibition, and shut down the grocery afterward. Today the building is still used as a tavern, the Sportsman's Lounge.

South Seas and palm trees was the fashion style during World War II. The Spot Tavern at 216 East Monroe Street in downtown Springfield sports the latest in 1941 decor. The old building, with its pressed metal ceiling and wooden balcony, has been camouflaged with Moderne "streamlined" bar and stools, grass-hut doorway and even a grass-skirted mannequin. The "God Bless America" banner and containers of beernuts (five cents) are incongruous but typical bar items. J.M. Fahey was the manager. The Spot apparently proved unpopular after the novelty wore off, for it appears in Springfield city directories only for 1939 and 1940.

Bars all over Springfield were modernizing in the 1930s and '40s, perhaps trying to shed their former saloon image and project a more respectable, club-like atmosphere. One of the liveliest, Johnnie Connor's Empire Saloon and Hotel, was no exception. Shown in this August 1950 photo, the bar—once the scene of drinking, betting, fighting and less savory activities, now looks positively sedate. While the old pressed ceilings and heating pipes remain, the walls have been covered with a composition material. A new lighted Art-Moderne back bar and Art-Deco ceiling lights appeared. The large-dial radio at far right let patrons tune into the latest baseball game broadcast.

Edward A. Ludwig, posing for this 1966 photo in Booker's Tavern, began tending bar in Springfield taverns about 1910. Ludwig had worked at Booker's for twenty-four years at the time of this photo.

Corner locations, with their high visibility, were popular sites for Springfield businesses, including taverns and saloons. The building in the northwest corner of Eleventh Street and South Grand Avenue was a prime example. It was used as a tavern as early as 1907 and operated under several names. George T. Booker put his name on the building about 1942 and his name remained on the door until 1975. The building has since reopened as a tavern. This photo shows Booker's as it appeared in 1948.

Moline's Tavern at the northwest corner of Eighth and Adams streets was typical of the many, long-running drinking establishments in downtown Springfield. Opened in 1924 during prohibition as a soft-drink stand and restaurant by Henry Moline, it became a tavern after the repeal of the Eithteenth Amendment. Moline owned and operated his business for thirty-three years. Henry Moline (second from right) is pictured with his staff inside the tavern in this circa 1931 photo.

Teen Hangouts

Young people were once expected to work long hours at home and to begin jobs at an early age. As the twentieth century progressed, students stayed in school longer and had continually more free time. Those between the ages of thirteen and eighteen were first officially categorized as teenagers in the twentieth century. This was the first time this age group had been thought of as distinct. They were ascribed particular identity-traits and encouraged to join into activities together. After school these increasingly independent youngsters frequented soda fountains, short-order restaurants, and other places. Diana's Sweet Shop, Alvey's Pool Hall, Bea's Ice Cream Shop, and the old "Top Deck" in the basement of the Y.M.C.A. were all popular downtown gathering spots in the 1930s and '40s. Neighborhood places favored by students included Priddy's Inn on South Sixth, Coutrakon's on North Grand, the Sugar Bowl on South Grand, and Buck's Campus Inn on Lewis Street.

By the 1950s, teens seemed inseparable from the automobile and traveled all over town. Certain businesses catered almost solely to teens—especially the new drive-in restaurants. The Icy Root Beer, Steak 'n Shake, Don's Drive-In, Russell's Drive-In, Triple Treat and, later, McDonalds, were all designed around the car. Teenage "hangouts" have become a permanent part of Springfield entertainment.

"Meet me at Coots" was a popular greeting at Lanphier High School during the 1940s and '50s. Coutrakon's Confectionery was located on North Grand Avenue between Eighth and Ninth streets, conveniently next to the Pantheon Theater—another popular teenage gathering spot. Shown here in 1945, Coutrakon's sports the victory "V" of World War II.

Homer Sharp purchased Ruth's Cafe at Eleventh Street and Enos Avenue about 1945. Students from nearby Concordia Seminary and workers from the International Shoe Factory supplied a steady lunchtime crowd. Sharp gradually began to stress recreation over food at the cafe and offered one of the first shuffleboards in town. He later added pinball machines and juke box. Full meals were reduced to short orders as customers came mostly for the games. Beginning with two used pool tables, Sharp eventually built a 70' x 35' addition for a full pool room where celebrity tournaments were held. This group of teens from 1957 include a would-be James Dean and two seminary students.

Don's Sangamon Dairy Drive-in at 2100 South MacArthur Avenue was most popular with Sacred Heart, Griffin, and Springfield High School students. Hamburgers and milkshakes were the cuisine of choice in this scene from about 1960.

The Icy Root Beer had two drive-ins, one at Fifth Street and South Grand Avenue, and this one at North Grand and Rutledge avenues. The modern "California" design includes a long covered carport with electric call-boxes for placing orders. Carhops brought the food to the customer's car.

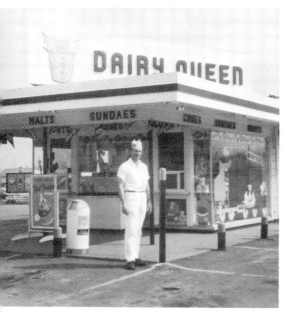

Russell's Pizza Drive-Inn was a favorite with Feitshans and Lanphier high school students in the mid to late 1950s. It was operated by the Yannone family and located at 301 North Dirksen Parkway (then Thirty-first Street). Note the sign pointing out the latest convenience—a telephone, which could be used without leaving your car.

When Gilbert and Frances Stein opened their Illini Dairy Queen franchise at 2540 South MacArthur Boulevard in about 1952, the street was already well on its way to becoming a major city traffic artery. Teens in cars crowded the parking lot in the early 1960s. By decade's end the business expanded and moved next door north, where it remains today.

Like the beach house at Lake Springfield, the city park pavilions offered a place for a snack and soda, favorite teen food. This 1962 photo shows the Washington Park concession stand. "Stop past when you're driving in the park," said the ads.

Taverns, Boardinghouses, and Five-Star Hotels

Some of Springfield's earliest buildings were taverns where people could find lodgings. From the primitive conditions at early Springfield inns and taverns, such as Archer Herndon's Indian Queen Hotel and Andrew Elliot's Elk-horn Tavern, to the elegant rooms and lavish trappings at the Leland, Saint Nicholas, and Abraham Lincoln hotels, Springfield's numerous hotels have provided visitors, both famous and unknown, with a place to stay the night.

Even before the state legislature voted to move the state capital to Springfield in 1837, construction on the American House, Springfield's first important hotel, was started by town founder Elijah Iles. When it was completed in 1838, the American House provided a suitable place for legislators to stay and dine. Other hotels soon followed. By the late 1850s, an average of nine hotels were operating in the city, not to mention numerous boarding houses. The Saint Nicholas, opened in 1856, was one of the longest-running hotels in Springfield, lasting over one hundred years. The original Leland Hotel and Revere House were built in the mid 1860s.

Springfield directories of the 1880s list more than twenty hotels. Ownership changed frequently, as did the names of the establishments.

One of the important features of the hotels in Springfield was the cuisine. Many, such as the Saint Nicholas and Leland hotels, were known for the excellent food served in their large dining rooms as well as their lounges. Springfield's large hotels also provided patrons with bars, clubrooms, ballrooms, barbershops, and magazine and cigar stands.

After the turn of the century, many of the older Springfield hotels were either closed or turned into boarding houses. The big hotels were remodeled or rebuilt. A new Leland was constructed after a fire in 1908. The St. Nicholas received a six-story annex in 1910 and an eleven-story addition in 1925. The Abraham Lincoln Hotel, built in 1925, was known as "Springfield's Million-Dollar Hotel." Like some of its predecessors, the Abraham Lincoln went through financial difficulties during much of its existence. By 1970 Springfield's oldest, grandest downtown hotels no longer existed. Changes in society and low occupancy rates led to their closure. Cheaper, convenient motels and motor lodges at the edge of town took over much of their business.

Henry R. Ramstetter built the Brilliant House on the northeast corner of Fifth and Jefferson streets in 1865. A combination saloon and hotel, it was typical of the smaller hotels that served Springfield throughout the nineteenth century. Though considered primarily a hotel, the Brilliant House was also listed as a boarding house in later years. Many other Springfield hotels changed to boarding houses as they aged. This photo was taken circa 1890. Pete's Cafe was the last occupant of the building before it was demolished in 1985.

The American House, built by Elijah Iles, was Springfield's first important hostelry. Opened in late 1838, it was home to many state legislators during the legislative season as well as to important visitors during their stay in Springfield. One of Springfield's early social gathering places, the American House was the scene of countless balls and parties. Several of the city's early musical and theatrical events were staged here. The hotel passed through numerous owners before being purchased by Rheuna Lawrence in 1881. The building was torn down and a new one put up in its place. John Bressmer leased the building and moved his famous mercantile business there.

This artistic impression of the Revere House on the northwest corner of Fourth and Washington streets in 1874, shows tree-lined sidewalks and a hotel bus that brought customers to and from Springfield train stations. The Revere House was built circa 1867-68 by Joel S. Johnson. Johnson was also the proprietor of the City Hotel, located right across the street, which he had sold to the Chenery family in 1855 and was renamed the Chenery House.

The modest Grand Hotel at 109 North Seventh did not quite live up to its name. At the time it was built in 1906, it was one of the many small hotels in the downtown area. The Queen Anne facade with its decorative turret and bay windows gave the building its distinctive charm. But a view overlooking the city jail on the north and the hangings that took place there may have chilled patron enthusiasm and prevented it from being as successful as it might have been. By the 1960s and '70s it served as substandard housing for many low-income residents. Today the jail is gone but the old hotel building has been restored for use as the city's Visitors Bureau, part of a small collection of restored downtown Springfield buildings.

The Governor Hotel, at 418 East Jefferson, held a grand opening on August 29, 1958, as a totally remodeled and up-graded facility. The "Organ Grinder Room" was a popular gathering spot. The Governor became home to many legislators when the General Assembly was in session. Previously it was the Empire Hotel operated by Johnny Connors and had acquired an impressive list of names in its guest book, including aviation hero Charles Lindbergh. Many of the celebrities playing the Orpheum stayed at the Empire, too. The Governor has once again changed names and is today the Capital Plaza Hotel.

109

Leland Hotel

One of Springfield's best-known hotels, the Leland was built in 1866 by a group of Springfield businessmen who saw the need for a large and elegant hostelry. The Leland was completed and ready for business on the first day of 1867. The hotel was leased to Simeon Leland & Company of New York, a well-known hotel manager. Horace S. Leland bought out his Uncle Simeon's interest in the venture and, with his brother-in-law, Noble B. Wiggins, formed the firm of Horace S. Leland & Company. The Leland Hotel became noted for its elegant dining room and for the popular balls and dances held there. Many famous personages, including several U. S. presidents, were guests of the Leland Hotel. Like its counterpart, the Saint Nicholas, which was known for its affiliation with the Democratic Party, the Leland was the unofficial political headquarters for the Republican Party in downstate Illinois.

Noble Bates Wiggins became the proprietor of th Leland in 1889 after the death of Horace Leland. nine-story hotel was rebuilt in 1911 after a disastrou fire destroyed much of the old building in 1908. At tha time, the Wiggins family sold the business to a group c Springfield businessmen. The Leland reopened for busi ness in 1913 and was leased to Edward O. Perry, wh managed it until 1919 when his son Edward S. took ove The Perry family eventually bought the hotel in 1920 and retained it until 1947, when it was sold to J.F Nevin. The hotel was leased, bought, and sold severa times in the next two decades. Its name was changed ii 1965 to the Leland Motor Hotel, which reflected the nev parking facilities adjacent to the downtown hotel. I ceased operation as a hotel in 1970. Today the Lelan building houses the offices of the Illinois Commerc Commission.

Colonel Noble Bates Wiggins was connected with the Leland Hotel first as steward, then as a partner, and finally as sole owner up to his death in 1901. Wiggins was known for his courtesy and integrity. Under his management, the Leland Hotel became widely known as a first-rate establishment. Wiggins is pictured here in 1880.

Employees of the Leland Hotel's dining room, clad in handsome uniforms, stand patiently for this photo taken in 1892. Hundreds of people were served daily in this dining room.

This photograph shows the old Leland Hotel before it was destroyed by fire in 1908. The five-story structure stood on the northwest corner of Sixth and Capitol streets and was known for the closed-door political deals commonly made there during legislative sessions.

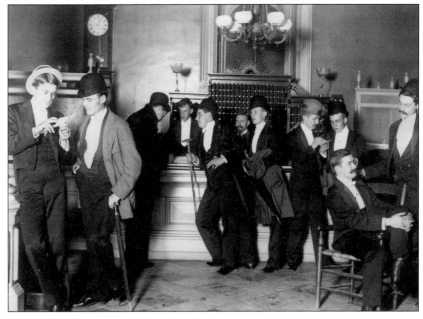

This 1889 scene at the Leland Hotel Lobby was captured by Springfield attorney and amateur photographer Will Patton. These "young society gentlemen" are in a carefully poised revelry with the old clock showing 12:45 a.m. They are, left to right, Temple Smith, Philip "Bart" Warren, Will Shutt, Horace Wiggins, Henry Walker, Carl Batchelder, night clerk at hotel; Fred Merritt, Waldo Reed, George Buck, George Wetherbee, who is seated in front, and Will Vredenburgh.

As this 1933 menu shows, patrons of the Leland Hotel's restaurant had a wide selection of seafood, meats, vegetables, side dishes, and desserts to choose from for their Christmas dinner.

Springfield hotels and restaurants were known for their baked goods, which were made fresh daily on site. The baking staff of the old Leland, led by Henry W. Zeppenfeld (at left), is shown in this photo from about 1913. It was also in the Leland kitchens where the locally-famous horseshoe sandwich was invented.

When it opened in 1956, the Red Lion Tavern at the Leland Hotel promised to transport diners back to Merry Olde England. Bartenders, waitresses, and busboys were garbed in period costumes. Interior decorations included armor, shields, swords, and axes, as well as stuffed and mounted animals. An open hearth at the far end of the room gave diners a clear view of the chef as he prepared their meals.

The Leland Hotel's ballroom was the scene of many balls and dances as well as other functions. In this 1947 photo, members of the Dad's Club are entertained.

This photo shows the Leland Hotel on a bright and sunny June day in 1955. To the west of the main building is the hotel annex, built in 1896. When the annex opened, it featured "the latest and best furniture and was equipped with electric lighting, steam heat, and a complete system of electric call bells."

The Saint Nicholas
Hotel as it appeared
in the 1950s.

One of Springfield's longest operating hotels was the Saint Nicholas, located on the southeast corner of Fourth and Jefferson streets. The original building was constructed in 1856 by J.D. Freeman. In 1862, John McCreery, in partnership with James Sponsler, took over ownership and management of the hotel. Five years later McCreery bought out his partner and assumed sole ownership. McCreery managed the hotel until his retirement, followed by his son John H. McCreery, who ran it until his death in 1920. During the younger McCreery's tenure, an annex was built south of the main hotel, which still stands. In 1920, management and ownership passed to the Bartholf family and F.E. Shuster. In 1925 the original section of the hotel facing Fourth Street was demolished and an eleven-story addition was constructed. The remainder of the original hotel was later demolished and the two-story building facing Jefferson Street was built. The hotel was leased to N.D. West and his son J.E. West in 1943.

The Saint Nicholas was well-known in the Midwest for its food and as the downstate headquarters of the Democratic Party. In 1953, three St. Louis businessmen, O.P. Greathouse, Carl E. Roessler, and Carl Stifel, purchased the hotel for $700,000. In 1967, it was sold again to another group of investors headed by Chicago stockbroker Norman A. Wolf. Throughout much of its existence the Saint Nicholas was kept modern through various remodelings and upgrades. The Saint Nicholas was in the limelight nationally in 1970 when $800,000 in cash was found in shoeboxes and a bowling bag in the fifth-floor suite of the late Paul Powell, Illinois Secretary of State. Money problems forced the owners of the hotel to close and file for bankruptcy in 1973. The Saint Nicholas was bought by Springfield builder Sam Sgro and reopened in 1974. Financial difficulties continued for the Saint Nicholas and it closed permanently in 1977. In recent years it reopened as the Saint Nicholas Apartments and still offers fine food and accommodations.

While the Saint Nicholas Hotel was a popular place from the first, it wasn't until 1867, a decade after its opening, that John McCreery (pictured here) gained sole control of the hotel and it achieved financial stability. Under McCreery, and later his son, John H., the hotel expanded several times. John McCreery's photograph was taken at the time he was mayor of Springfield in the early 1880s.

Even though it was in one of the two finest hotels in Springfield in the 1890s, the dining room of the St. Nicholas Hotel was somewhat spartan in appearance. An 1892 description notes the St. Nick boasted most modern conveniences (such as an elevator and steam heat), but evidently lavish interior decorating was not yet common in large hotel dining rooms.

The original portion of the St. Nicholas Hotel, which opened in 1857 on the corner of Fourth and Jefferson streets, can still be seen in this circa 1922 photo.

Under the leadership of John H. McCreery the St. Nicholas Annex was built in 1912 (the building with bay windows). Plans for an eleven-story structure that would take up the space from the Annex north to the corner of Jefferson Street were made in the early 1920s. Construction on the first half of the building was finished in 1925, but the Great Depression halted completion of the twin half of the building. In 1939 the original 1856 building was demolished and a two-story addition built. Photo circa 1955.

A new dining room facility at the St. Nicholas Hotel in 1952 featured a decorating theme using forest scenes, artificial trees, brick, and cypress paneling. A contest was held to name the room, with William J. Millar's entry "The Glade" winning.

Shown here in this circa 1892 photo is the remodeled lobby in the original hotel building of the St. Nick. Gas lights illuminated the decorative ceiling. Stencil work decorated the wall above the mirror, which is surrounded by advertisements from local businesses.

Abraham Lincoln Hotel

Springfield in the mid-1920s was ripe for a third large hotel downtown, thought C. Hayden Davis. After all, Springfield was centrally located between St. Louis and Chicago, it was a part of the new hard road system which attracted automobile travelers, it was a railroad center, it had a tourist draw, and it was, of course, the state capital. Investors agreed. Architectural plans were drawn up by Helmle & Helmle and carried out by Caldwell-Evans Construction Company with hardly a change or delay. In October 1925, the Abraham Lincoln Hotel took its place alongside the Leland and Saint Nicholas as a leading city hotel. Located at Fifth and Capitol streets, the "Abe" was then considered one of the best downstate hotels. A ballroom, private dining rooms, banquet rooms, state suites, and a reported "Key Club for gamblers" provided entertaining for Springfieldians and out-of-towners. The hotel even had a radio station, which took advantage of the live entertainment performing there. The hotel was also locally famous for all the political planning and maneuvering that took place in its private dining rooms and the Club Lido bar, as well as for refusing to serve black state legislator Corneal Davis in 1943. Davis spent the night sleeping on a wooden bench in the GM&O station.

The thirteen-story, 300-room Abraham Lincoln Hotel was built in 1925 at a cost of $1.4 million. It received a harsh financial setback during the Great Depression, and was plagued by money woes over much of its existence.

Visitors entered the main lobby from a wide staircase, which led to the second floor, where a convenience counter, main dining room, and lounges were located. The "Abe" Lincoln was beginning a short period of prosperity at the time this 1937 lobby view was shot. Eight governors made use of the hotel and rooms were rented to presidents Herbert Hoover, Harry S. Truman, Richard Nixon, and Wendell Wilke, as well as to famous entertainers.

Visitors to the second floor of the Abe Lincoln were greeted by an Italian style decor in deep blue. Tall, oval-top windows provided a backdrop for an outdoor sunken garden effect in the main lounging area.

During World War II when the hotel was at its most prosperous, business began to decline the building. The rationing of materials prevented needed repairs. During the 1950s several owners attempted to modernize the hotel to attract more customers, as seen in this 1958 view of the remodeled lobby. But to no avail. The doors closed on the hotel in 1964.

Abraham Lincoln Hotel

Sunday

December 17, 1978

8:30 a.m.

625 pounds of dynamite

Seven sharp blasts

Ten seconds

Rubble

Parking lot

117

Roadside Respites

While Springfield hotels provided dining rooms, ball-rooms, and bar space for local residents and the traveling public, the motel generally offered only inexpensive sleeping quarters. But it did provide accommodations for the thousands of motoring tourists who visited Springfield annually. The Lincoln sites, the Illinois State Fair, and the government buildings had drawn tourists to Springfield since before the turn of the century. With the coming of the automobile and hard roads, families found it easier to take vacations. For those who didn't care to pull over and set up camp in a farmer's field, the auto-camp developed. A clean place with a bed was all that was expected. But after World War II, tourists began to look for more in their overnight lodgings and competition between motels induced many of them to take on a resort-like appearance—providing playgrounds, restaurants, and eventually swimming pools. Hotel amenities, such as luxury suites and live entertainment, soon filtered into some of the larger chain-operated motels. What had once been popular "mom and pop" businesses began to disappear, replaced by larger chains.

The Capitol Motel at 4129 Peoria Road along Business Route 66 was ready to attract tourists headed to the Lincoln sites in the 1950s. The Capitol offered "Ultra modern" rooms, which usually meant air-conditioners, private tile baths, steam heat or electric heaters, and sometimes radio and TV.

Individual cabins were a common feature of many of the early motels, such as these "Octo" Cabins of the late 1930s located at 2739 West Grand Avenue South (today's MacArthur Boulevard near the Wabash curve).

The Lamp Liter Tourist Lodge, located south of Springfield along Route 66, began with this motel building, a few plantings, and a rustic fence around a yard. As the trees grew it soon took on a secluded resort-like atmosphere and expanded to include dining facilities that attracted Springfield residents as well as tourists.

The Lazy A Motel, 2840 Peoria Road, was built in 1949 to accommodate travelers along the now legendary Route 66. It had a southwestern theme to set it apart from the many other Route 66 motels. Because the Lazy A evokes the Route 66 era, it has been listed on the National Register of Historic Places.

One of Springfield's earlier motels, the Highway Hotel, 1305 Wabash, had changed its name to Highway Motel by 1954. The word "motel" (motor hotel) came into common use in the 1950s and the terms "tourist courts" and "tourist lodge" were dropped.

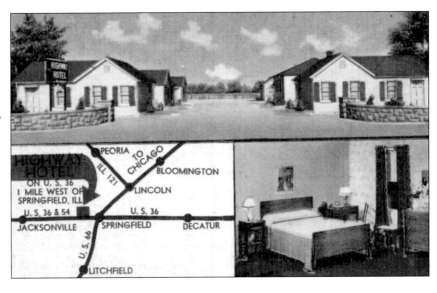

Fleck's Motel opened in 1939 using a children's playhouse for its first motel unit. Located at the corner of Bruns Lane and Jefferson Street, the tree-shaded area initially attracted truck drivers who wanted a place to pull over and sleep. That led Frank J. Fleck to develop his motel business. A "walking Lincoln"—the motel's symbol—was a familiar site for many years.

While many of the motels were on Route 66, each of the highways around Springfield had its share. The Sunset Motel was on the old Decatur hard road, Route 36.

119

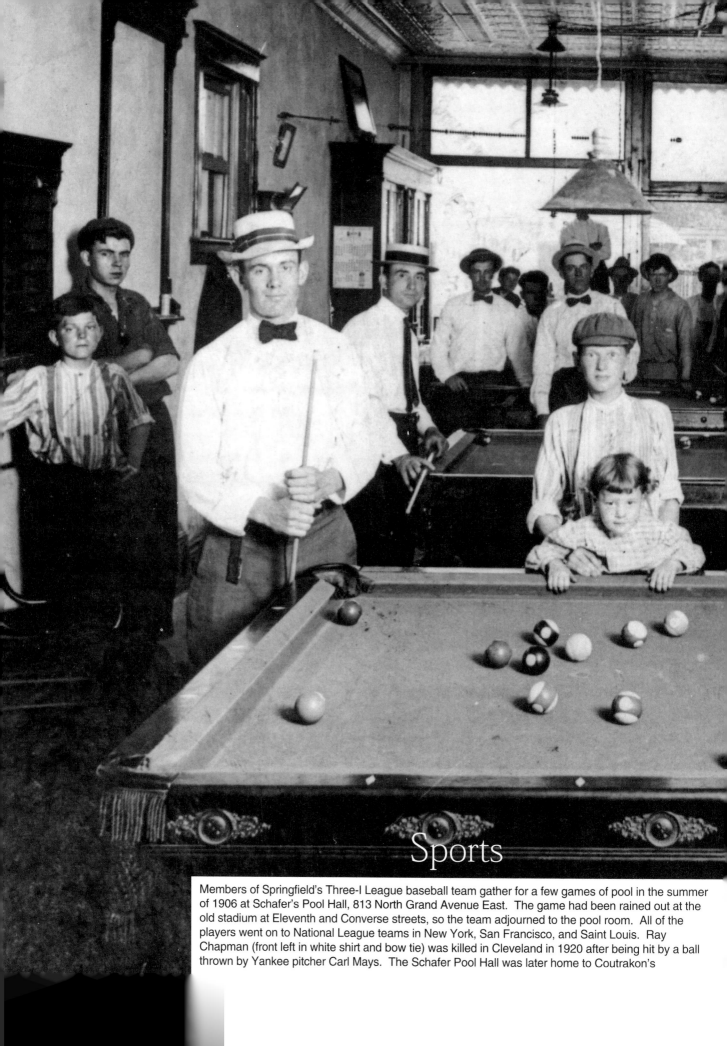

Sports

Members of Springfield's Three-I League baseball team gather for a few games of pool in the summer of 1906 at Schafer's Pool Hall, 813 North Grand Avenue East. The game had been rained out at the old stadium at Eleventh and Converse streets, so the team adjourned to the pool room. All of the players went on to National League teams in New York, San Francisco, and Saint Louis. Ray Chapman (front left in white shirt and bow tie) was killed in Cleveland in 1920 after being hit by a ball thrown by Yankee pitcher Carl Mays. The Schafer Pool Hall was later home to Coutrakon's

The Strike Zone

As early as the 1850s, a "bowling saloon" was advertised in Springfield city directories. Downtown Springfield was the location of a half dozen bowling alleys by the early 1900s—Arion Club Alleys, Clint Gordy's, the Grand Alleys, New Capitol Alleys, and others. Bowling became a favorite urban sport after 1900. Unlike tennis or golf which required daylight, workers could play in lighted buildings after dark. The game, says recreation historian Foster Rhea Dulles, has particularly attracted "...salesmen, office employees, retail clerks, factory hands, and other skilled workers." The automatic pinsetter made it possible to open large alleys with as many as two-dozen lanes under one roof. Springfield Bow located at First and Adams streets, featured up-to-th minute bowling technology when it opened in 1941. Th Knights of Columbus and Elks Club buildings also ha alleys. Businesses, clubs, and organizations sponsore their own teams for league play. Even the Orpheur Theater had its own bowling alleys. By 1956 nearly 10 leagues played at six city lanes.

The Springfield Women's Bowling Association wa founded in 1929, and one charter member, Clar Bogenschutz, was still active in the League in th 1970s. Springfield's Bowling Hall of Fame honors ou standing bowlers from each generation.

These unidentified gentlemen bowlers were Springfield City champions in 1931. The men proudly display their trophy and medals along with artfully arranged ball and pins.

The Knights of Columbus new club building offered a basement bowling alley in the 1920s. After World War II, the lanes were completely modernized and automatic pinsetters installed. The lanes remained a popular sport for league playing during the 1950s and '60s. This photo was made in 1947.

The Spillway, 1120 Sangamon Avenue, was the first of the post-war bowling alleys. It was completed in 1946 and followed by Strike and Spare (1958), King Pin (1960), and Town and Country (1961) lanes. The Spillway was destroyed in a spectacular fire in 1984.

A Springfield bowling team from the 1950s poses with its score-card advertising Rheingold beer.

Fitzpatrick Lumber Company owner James R. Fitzpatrick sponsored women's baseball and bowling teams. A Fitzpatrick Lumberjacks women's bowling team is shown in this 1950s photo.

Pleasure Wheels

About 1876, high-wheel bicycles were introduced in the United States. Enthusiasm for riding the new invention was so strong that in a little more than a decade there were an estimated 100,000 people who regularly cycled. Bicycle clubs were organized in every city and town, including Springfield. The Capital City Cycling Club was organized September 23, 1887, and soon had almost 100 members. The club's headquarters occupied much of the third floor of the Hay Building at sixth and Washington streets and included library/reading, billiard and pool rooms. A silver loving cup was presented to the winner of the club's annual race. Besides those in the club, noted an 1896 story, "there are several hundred ladies, gentlemen, boys, and girls who glide over the smoothly paved streets of Springfield every day. Famed temperance leader and feminist Frances E. Willard advocated that women master bicycle riding as a "metaphor" for life. The principles by which one masters life, marriage, and family." The coming of the automobile as personal transportation pushed cycling from a prime form of transportation and recreation to a sport of children and a few enthusiasts through most of the twentieth century.

The 1890s were a time of a great cycling "craze." In Springfield, Capital City Cycling Club members competed with cyclers from other communities. This 1891 view shows riders at a meet held in Springfield. Cyclists came from Jacksonville, Quincy, and Peoria and posed at the front of the State Capitol for this photo. In the front row are Springfield residents Perry Jayne, A.J. Mester, Frank Hamilton (later City Commissioner), and later Mayor Hal Smith (In white hat at far right).

Cycling for pleasure and transportation was also a popular Springfield pastime. Sisters Loretta and Edna Keefner have donned their brother's clothes (and bicycle) for this amusing photo, taken about 1921. The scene was in the back of the family's home at 811 South Twelfth Street.

Alfred Mester was an avid cyclist and participated in most the of the Capital City Cycling Club's competitions. Here he is shown wearing a cycling "duster" in 1905. Mester's grandson today owns the restored bicycle.

Children caught the bicycle fever early. Young Gwynne Rohrer peddles an early-model tricycle in this photo taken about 1906. The house in the background is at 314 South Seventh Street, today the site of the Municipal Plaza in front of City Hall.

In the gasoline age, motor power was added to bicycles to create the motorized-cycle or motorcycle. Chester Sweet is shown on his 1914 model Indian Motorcycle.

A new bicycle has been a child's dream for generations. This tempting display was parked in front of Sears Roebuck and Company's Springfield store at 621 East Adams Street in about 1931 or '32.

Skating in the Moonlight

Roller-skating was made fashionable by New York and Newport society leaders in the 1860s. Its popularity was instantaneous and skating rinks opened in nearly every town by the 1870s. Springfield's earliest-known skating rink opened in the old First Baptist Church on the southwest corner of Seventh and Adams streets in the 1870s. The church building—which also once held the official city clock—perfectly-suited a skating rink. Other large spaces, like the old city Market House at Eighth and Capitol streets, served as roller rinks, as did several of the public "halls" including the Central Music Hall at Fourth and Jefferson streets.

But without a doubt the most famous skating rink was Moonlight Gardens at Wabash Avenue and Chatham Road. Roy Dexhimer Sr. opened a service station there and followed with a dance hall and custard stand. The dance hall—Moonlight Gardens—was very successful and was converted to a skating rink in the mid 1930s. The new rink continued to be a popular gathering and recreational spot for young people from Springfield and surrounding areas. "Drinking of alcoholic beverages is strictly prohibited at all times," according to a 1959 news story, "with the result that rowdyism never occurs and is never permitted." City buses brought customers to the door. The building was redecorated several times to keep in style with changing fashions. Moonlight Gardens closed in 1965.

A postcard view of Moonlight Gardens on the northeast corner of Wabash Avenue and Chatham Road, circa 1950.

Prizewinning skating dancers Minnette Mester and Jimmy Young take a few turns around Moonlight Gardens' highly polished floor in 1943.

Moonlight Gardens was a member of the Roller Skating Rink Operators' Association. The Association sponsored sanctioned events and reviews during the 1940s. This 1941 photograph shows Moonlight Gardens' "Moonlight Waltz Club" dancers posed here in front of an elaborately draped, starred, and festooned backdrop.

The Courtly Sport

Tennis became a popular American recreation in the 1880s, at first a "gentle diversion of polite society, essentially for ladies and gentlemen." In 1890s, young gentlemen from local society introduced the game in Springfield back yards. Tennis racquets, nets, and lady spectators in the cool shade were all the young men required. By the 1920s and '30s the game had become far more aggressive and competitive among both men and women. The latter now played "in dress which would have horrified their Victorian forebears—short-skirted, bare-legged," according to the historian Foster Dulles. Increasingly, Springfield parks opened tennis courts for public play—Washington, Iles, and Lincoln parks being early ones.

the 1890s tennis was much considered a refined pastime for gentlemen and ladies. These young men were members of Springfield's Eronian Dance Club, but also met regularly at members home to play tennis. This photo, taken about 1897, shows, in the front row: Larue Vredenburgh, Louis G. Coleman, Leonard Wood. Second row seated: Nicholas R. Jones, Ridgely Hudson, J. Bunn Henkle and third row, John H. Radish, George E. Keys, George Oliver, James A. Jones, and John C. Lanphier Jr.

By the 1920s tennis had become an extremely popular game and boasted stars like the legendary Bill Tilden. Tennis "whites" were de rigeur and the sport was offered at the city's public high school. This 1923 photo shows Springfield High School's tennis team. Left to right, Charles McGovin, Arthur Buffington, Coach P.C. Buley, Howard Buley, and Paul Welch.

Washington Park had tennis courts for public play as early as 1910. The park's fieldhouse and courts are shown in the 1950s.

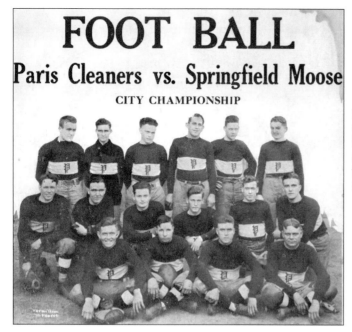

FOOT BALL
Paris Cleaners vs. Springfield Moose
CITY CHAMPIONSHIP

Local football teams were in regular play in turn-of-the-century Springfield. Several businesses sponsored their own, including Paris Cleaners, whose team is shown here in the 1915 hand-bill for city championship play.

Without a doubt J.R. "Bud" Fitzpatrick has the honor of sponsoring the greatest variety of sporting teams in Springfield. One of the shortest-lived was the Fitzpatrick soccer team, shown here in 1947. Kneeling in the front row are Fred Stone, Ed Mullen, John Cooney, Jim Forrest, and Ernie Cramer. Standing in the back row are William Stone, Sr., Fred Otta, H. Sablotny, William Stone, Pat Rodgers, Joe Parkinson, Jim Rodgers, Henry Matrisch, Adolph Matrisch, and John Sablotny.

The sport of soccer in Springfield has recently gained exceptional popularity. However Springfield soccer teams were on the scene as early as the 1940s. Springfield Mayor John W. "Buddy" Kapp, Junior (second from left), stand on a soccer field among players of the Fitzpatrick Lumberjacks soccer team in 1947.

The Early Days of "Hoops"

Basketball was developed at the Springfield, Massachusetts, YMCA in 1891. "Y's" throughout the country introduced the new game to their communities, including Springfield. For most of its early life, basketball was played strictly as an amateur sport. State high-school basketball tournaments became major community events, especially in the Midwest where "March Madness" is still an annual rite of spring. City high school teams have been competing statewide since the turn of the century. Springfield even had its own professional basketball team, the Illinois Express, for a short time in late 1980s. Though the Express was short-lived, Springfield maintains an overwhelming enthusiasm for the sport.

Springfield's Y.M.C.A. was founded in 1874 and promoted "gymnasium work...for the masses rather than for the few." Besides calisthenics, marching, exercise machines, baseball, volleyball, and track, the "Y" sponsored its own basketball team. The 1911-12 team poses here for the camera. Players, we are told, learned "the value of physical exercise, of clean play, fair play, and team play...leadership.. the ability to hold fast, even in a losing game, and to keep on fighting and always fairly, even when beaten, a knowledge which stands them in good stead in the business life."

The Fitzpatrick Lumberjacks basketball team won the coveted Springfield Municipal League Championship in 1943-44. The team is shown before practice in the spring of 1945 with sponsor J.R. "Bud" Fitzpatrick. From left to right are: Bud Hickey, Larry Markie, Carl Wenke, unknown, unknown, Leroy Bennett, unknown, Walt David, unknown, Harry Moats, and J.R. Fitzpatrick.

Many companies encouraged sports teams as a way for employees to build camaraderie and "team spirit" within the company. Central Illinois Public Service company was no exception. Its 1929-30 basketball team consisted of (front, left to right): Floyd Vannatta, J.R. Broderick, Alfred Mester, Jr., Arthur James, and back, left to right, James Cadagin, John Hunter (later CWLP commissioner), Preston Wilson (coach), Ralph Williams, and William Barber (captain).

Hot Wheels, Fast Tracks

Horse racing was popular in Springfield from its first days. A private race track was superseded by a new grandstand and track at the state fairgrounds in the 1890s. In the early 1900s, the first automobile races were held on that track. In 1905, driver Barney Oldfield, on a "barnstorming circuit," raced his famous Green Dragon car at the track, and again in 1910. Regular races were held with local drivers competing. One of these men, LaRue Vredenburgh, was killed when his Stoddard Dayton overturned in 1910. A new grandstand and track opened for the 1927 fair and in 1934 the first AAA, 100-mile National Championship race premiered. This race made the track famous nationwide. Numbers of Indianapolis drivers raced in Springfield as a popular part of the "Indy" circuit. The United States Auto Club (USAC) took over from AAA as sponsor for the races and gave Springfield a reputation as a "racing town". Springfield's famous mile track hosted "leaden-footed pilots...the cream of America daring dirt-track experts," according to a 1940 new story. The best-known private track in central Illinoi was Shaheen's Springfield Speedway at Clear Lak Avenue and Thirty-first Street. Opened in 1947 by Jo Shaheen, the Speedway offered USAC-sanctione midget races on the dirt track. Shaheen was so popula among drivers that they recommended him as consu tant to the Houston Astrodome when the owners set u a track there in the 1960s. In the 1950s and '60 Shaheen also held stock-car races including the popula "powder puff" competition, which featured only wome drivers. Lady racers like Mrs. Suzie Powers, a "soft-spo ken thirty-two-year-old grandmother" was one femal driver in the 1950s and '60s who still got the jitter before each race. "I shake all over until I let out m clutch as the race starts. Then I'm all right."

Every race can mean a possible crash. This scene from the 1930s shows the grim spectacle of a "midget" car accident at the state fairgrounds.

The Illinois State Fair was canceled during World War II, and AAA National Championship racing did not return until 1947. This photo from that year shows the blur of winner Myron Fohrs' car (at left) as it speeds around the track. There was great excitement at the return of championship racing to the city. Sports promoter Bud Fitzpatrick managed to raise an $8,500 purse for the winner. The race was held September 19th.

Springfield Speedway owner Joe Shaheen and sports promoter J.R. Fitzpatrick are shown (at left) in this photo from the 1950s. These two, along with William Menghini, were leaders in promoting auto racing in Springfield in the 1940s and '50s.

Springfield track owner Joe Shaheen is shown at his raceway standing between drivers Harry Myers (left) and Rex Easton (right). The photo was taken about 1950.

Shaheen's Springfield Speedway closed in 1988 and was replaced with a branch bank and shopping center, but the state fair races continue today.

Soap-box Derby

Soap-box derby racing was a fad from the 1930s through the 1950s. Young boys built and raced their own cars. Springfield's first derby was held in 1940, sponsored by the *Illinois State Register* and Bates Chevrolet. The races were generally held at Douglas Park. MacArthur Boulevard in front of the park was closed off for use as a race track.

Local winners had a chance to attend national championships sponsored by General Motors. The sport "fosters self-reliance, fair play, and the will to win"—skills "inherent in every American boy," proclaimed President Dwight Eisenhower in a promotional message for the derby. Springfield derby races were a thing of the past by the early 1960s.

Boys were impressed with the importance of fairness by serious-minded judges. Cars and their occupants were required to have their weights within stipulated ranges. Here Harold Stanton and his car (sponsored by Schlitt Supply Company) successfully "weigh-in" for the 1956 city race.

Derby drivers were encouraged to develop friendships among one another. This scene shows cars and drivers ready to race. Local sponsors ranged from Pillsbury Mills and Myers Brothers to Stehman Wrecking and Grizzell Insurance.

Drivers line up on MacArthur Boulevard. Douglas Park is at the left in this view facing south.

They're off! Racers are propelled
down the starting ramp and rush
north along the sloping brick-
paved MacArthur Boulevard.

At the opposite end of the street
awaits the finish line. The bright,
blue-plastic helmets could be
seen for long distances and
were issued "only to drivers,"
according to national rules.

David Burtle rushed to the
checkered flag in his Den
Chili Parlor sponsored car,
a winner in "Class B."

Tee Time

In 1895, C.D. Roberts, A.C. Brown, George Chatterton, M.W. Yates, Dr. E.E. Hagler, H.J. Palmer, J.D. Lloyd, and J.E. Cadwallader laid out a six-hole golf course at the Illinois State Fairgrounds. The gentlemen sunk coffee cans to act as cups. Out of this summer fad the Springfield Golf Club was formed. So great was local enthusiasm for the game that the club set up a nine-hole course in Milton Brown's thirty-acre pasture on West Lawrence Avenue and built a clubhouse there. This course was the nucleus of today's Pasfield Park course. Women quickly took up the game and, in time, the small course was soon overcrowded. In 1907 the Springfield Golf Club moved once again, one mile south, to what became Illini Country Club.

The first public course was opened at Bunn Park in 1912. The Grandview Country Club (later Oak Crest) followed in 1926. Pasfield's course was opened to the public in 1930 and Bergen Park had a course constructed. The latest-in-design, Lincoln Greens opened at Lake Springfield in the 1950s. Players from Illini competed with those from the public courses for City Championship titles. The Central Illinois Junior Tournament for young golfers was inaugurated in 1937 and later renamed the Bob Drysdale Golf Tournament, in honor of one of its founders. Today more than a dozen public and private courses in and around Springfield continue catering to this most popular of local sports.

An unidentifed golfer tees off at Illini Country Club about 1929.

Miss Elberta Thalia Smith, shown here at the Illini Golf Course about 1956, was one of the original members of the Illini Women Golfers Club, believed to be the oldest such group in the country. A passionate (and skilled) golfer, Miss Smith played well into her 80's, beating women half her age. Unfortunately group championship always eluded her.

Later used as a fieldhouse for Pasfield Park, this building was Springfield's first golf club house. It was built in 1900 in the old Milton Brown pasture at Lawrence Avenue near Chatham Road, where the Springfield Golf Club laid out its nine-hole course. A newspaper reminiscence of 1940 recalled that many players rode the old Governor Street trolley, got off near the "decrepit old fence of Krous [beer] Park on Amos Avenue," and walked west the remaining blocks. Golfers of the time wore no special clothing, often appearing on the links in business clothes.

Golf in Springfield proved equally popular with men and women. Here a group of would-be lady golfers gets a chance to improve their swings under the watchful eye of two male coaches. The scene is a spring Saturday morning at Springfield's Lanphier Ball Park in the late 1940s or early 1950s.

Golfers prepare to putt on a green of an unidentified Springfield golf course about 1931.

Miniature golf, although never followed with the consuming passion of the traditional game, has had a steady following in Springfield since the 1920s. The course could be built indoors giving frustrated golfers a place to practice putting on rainy days. This elaborate course was constructed by the Fitzpatrick Lumber Company in the old Knights of Columbus building the mid 1930s.

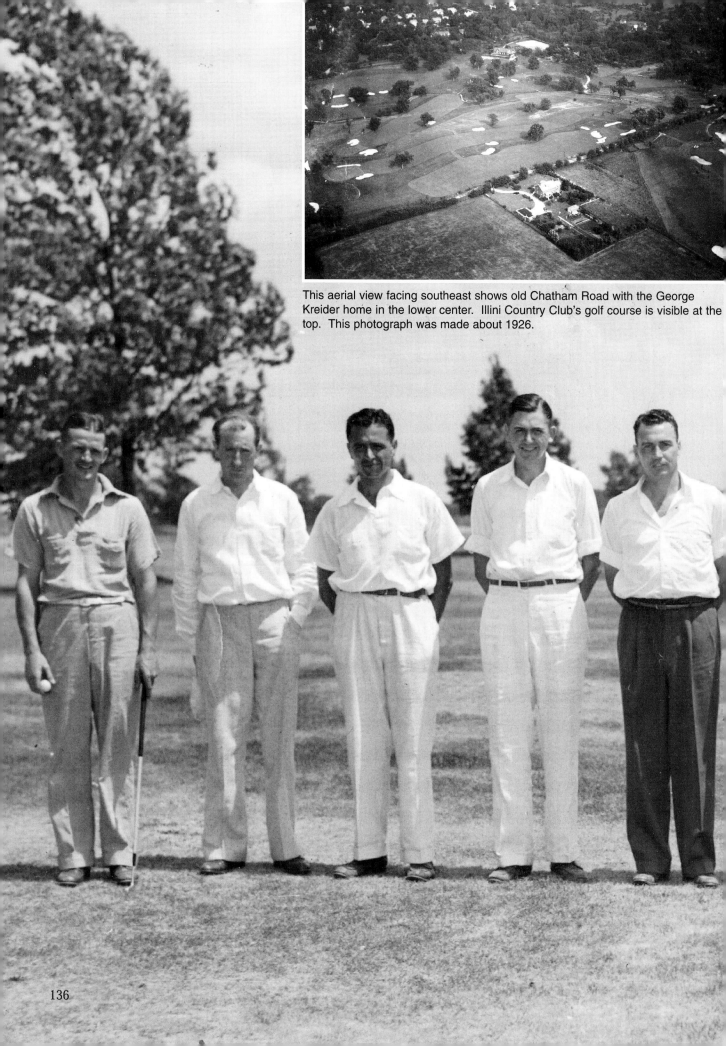

This aerial view facing southeast shows old Chatham Road with the George Kreider home in the lower center. Illini Country Club's golf course is visible at the top. This photograph was made about 1926.

Golf on the city's public courses became very popular in the 1920s and '30s. Eventually some of the teams played against the Illini Country Club for the city golf tournament. The men shown here played on the Bunn Park Golf Team in 1933. From left to right are Keeren Slowe, Jim Egan, Francis Schuster, Joe Patton, Eddie Charlton, Walt Repaske, John Watson, Noonie Pease, Bobby Charlton, Charles Nelch, and Barney Hoshman. Both Bob and Eddie Charlton were later inducted into the Springfield Sports Hall of Fame.

Illini Country Club's golf course is shown about 1960. The course was laid out on the rolling terrain formed by the Town Branch. The course remains in the same location along Chatham Road, which has gone from a farm lane to a major westside traffic artery.

Ringside in Springfield

Besides baseball, boxing was probably the most popular sporting event in Springfield during its heyday. Prizefighting, the forerunner of boxing, became popular in the 1880s with the rise in fame of John L. Sullivan, the Strong Boy of Boston. The popularity of amateur boxing began in Springfield in the late 1930s with Golden Gloves Competition. In 1937, Springfield firefighter Charles Lockhart converted the second floor of Engine House No. 5 at 1310 East Adams Street into a ring so young men could be trained to box. The *Illinois State Register* first sponsored the Golden Gloves Competition in the 1930s and '40s and J.R. Fitzpatrick's paper, the *Citizen's Tribune,* took over sponsorship from 1942 to 1956. The Illinois State Armory provided the perfect venue for bouts to be held. Large audiences attended the matches, which were popular into the late '50s when enthusiasm waned. Local champions in their weight classes moved on to the next level of competition.

Amateur boxing continued in Springfield with the formation of the Springfield Boxing Club by Clarence "Butch" Miller, Jack Cunningham, and Harold Bartnik in the early 1970s. Other teams would be sponsored through organizations such as the Springfield Housing Authority.

Spectators in folding chairs enjoy an outside boxing match between unknown opponents.

At the height of its popularity, boxing matches such as Golden Gloves competitions drew large crowds. The 1950 Golden Gloves championships held at the Illinois State Armory almost sold out. Teams from surrounding communities such as Jacksonville, Decatur, and Peoria would come to Springfield to compete.

A Golden Gloves competitor delivers a jarring punch to his opponent in this match.

This 1947 photo shows a group of young men training for Golden Gloves competition under the direction of Dave Barry at the Police Pals Training Center. Several other city clubs, such as Engine House No. 5, sent teams of boxers to compete in the Springfield championships. First row, left to right: Jack Gillespie, Mike Connoly. Second row: Bob DeFrates, Art Nolan, Donald Smith, Bob Fischer, Russ Killon, Jim Meyers, John Naylor. Third row: John Karlichek, George Stieren, Robert MacDonald, Frank Mazrim, Ralph Schafer, and Leo Zappa.

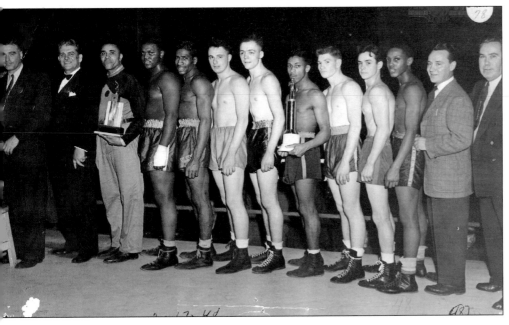

Pictured here in 1948 are eight champions of the Springfield Golden Gloves competition who went on to represent the city in the Chicago Tournament of Champions. Pictured left to right are Bill Steiger, Ed Lartz, Charles Lockhart Sr., Charles Lockhart Jr., William Cox, Dick Allen, Vern Peck, Richard Fortune, Johnny Naylor, Roger Fandel, and Frank Robinson. Charles Lockhart Sr. holds the team trophy won by the Engine House No. 5 team. Richard Fortune holds the Jim Fitzpatrick Memorial Trophy.

In the Batter's Box

(This excerpt is taken from a history of baseball in Springfield written by Richard West.)

Throughout its history, Springfield has gained a reputation as an in-and-out baseball town. It was only two years after the first professional team, the "Liberties," made its debut that the city was without a team, as the franchise moved to Peoria for one season, only to return in 1879. That new team, at best a semi-pro organization, played as the "Watch Factory," its sponsor. Semi-pro ball continued until 1884 when Springfield, along with seven other Midwestern communities from Ohio, Indiana, Iowa, Michigan, and Illinois, organized the Northwestern League giving the city its first representation in league play. This was short-lived as the league passed out of existence after only one year. This was due to the frequent reorganization of franchises and extensive travel. Springfield remained out of professional baseball until 1889 when the Mansfield, Ohio, team folded and moved here in mid-season, staying only that half a year. Semi-pro ball

predominated until 1893 when the "Kittens," featuring "Iron Man" Joe McGinnity (who later pitched for Baltimore, Brooklyn and the New York Giants during a stellar ten year major league career) was organized. The "Kittens" joined the professional ranks for only one season, remaining in existence for several years after that as a semi-pro operation.

In 1903, Springfield returned to professional baseball as a member of the Class B Three-I circuit when merchant Richard Kinsella took over the Joliet team in July and moved it to the capital. Kinsella's ownership lasted until 1911 when he pulled out prior to the start of the season, leaving the city without a team for one year before selling it to a local syndicate that operated through the 1914 season.

Professional baseball was absent from Springfield until a "fan's association" was organized in the winter of 1924. It raised enough money by February 1925 to begin construction of a stadium, Lanphier Park, which although much renovated, is substantially the same

This 1902 photo shows a group of baseball players from different Springfield teams. At this time, Springfield had two different city leagues, which had teams sponsored by businesses such as Myers Brothers, Franklin Life, Court of Honor, and organizations like the Capital City Cycling Club.

A Springfield baseball team poses for this circa 1916 photo at the ball field stadium at Eleventh and Black streets.

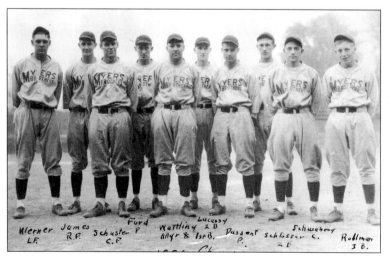

The Myers Brothers Clothiers defeated the St. Joseph's team, 8 to 7, at Reservoir Park to win the 1930 Springfield city baseball championship.

stadium today. Constructed at a cost of $49,000, the park was renamed Robin Roberts Stadium in 1977 to honor the former Springfield resident following his election to baseball's Hall of Fame.

Three-I resumed in 1925 with the Senators operating eventually under the sponsorship of the American Association Kansas City Blues until that relationship was discontinued following the 1931 season. On July 15, 1932, Springfield began its association with St. Louis baseball teams, becoming a Cardinal farm club when the Danville team moved here in a season shortened by the Great Depression. Since then, all Springfield teams have been either a Cardinal or St. Louis Browns farm club.

The following year, the team operated in the Mississippi Valley League and in 1934 was a member of the Class B Central League, which suspended operations after only two weeks of play on June 10.

The Three-I reorganized in 1935 with Springfield as a charter member, but the team folded following the end of the season due to heavy financial losses and remained out of baseball until 1938 when the Browns took over the franchise. With the exception of a three-year suspension caused by World War II travel restrictions, the Browns remained in the Three-I circuit until after the 1949 season when St. Louis President John MacWherter sold the team to Adam Pratt of Cedar Rapids, Iowa, who moved the team there.

Springfield tried one last time with professional baseball in 1950 when local businessman J.R. Fitzpatrick constructed a new stadium on the city's south side and operated a team in the Class D Mississippi Valley League, but that attempt failed to attract fan support and folded after its initial season.

Baseball was absent from Springfield until 1977 when New Orleans Pelican owner A. Ray Smith announced that the team would play a four-game exhibition series against the Evansville Triplets to test fan reaction to professional baseball. Attracting close to 13,000 fans during the short stand, Smith and the Springfield city council agreed to a five-year lease for the use of the stadium on October 25, with American Association approval of the shift coming on January 30, 1978. That same situation has continued to the present day.

1939 record book for the Springfield Browns team, which played in the Three-I League.

Alby Plain of Springfield was typical of the many local talented baseball players. Plain was a standout at Springfield High School and in the Springfield Municipal League. This 1944 photo shows him in the uniform of the Fitzpatrick Lumberjacks, a Springfield Municipal League team.

Springfield once had several Little League teams filled with boys who dreamed of making it to the "Big Leagues." This 1940s photo shows an unidentified Springfield Little League team.

141

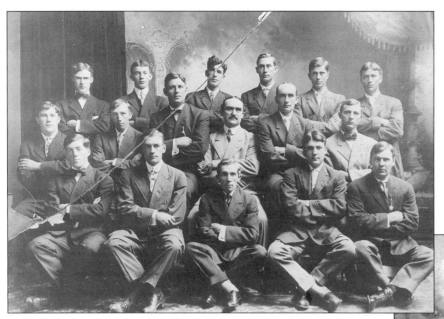

These men, dressed in their business suits, made up the 1910 Springfield Three-I League baseball team. Their owner, Richard Kinsella, is seated in the middle row, fourth from the left.

Walter Schaller (right) played for Springfield's Three-I League team as an outfielder. He later played for the Pacific Coast League team in San Francisco, California.

Former baseball team owner Richard Kinsella, throws out the first pitch for a Three-I game in the 1920s.

The Springfield Senators played the Bloomington Bloomers in a Three-I League game at Lanphier Park on opening day, April 28, 1927. Governor Len Small was on hand to throw out the opening pitch. The Senators defeated the Bloomers by a score of 20-2. This picture shows players, owners, and officials standing in front of the banner draped grandstand.

Richard Kimble of the Springfield Browns models the uniform worn in post World War II days.

Donald Barnes of St. Louis takes a swing at a pitch during the 1939 Three-I League baseball opener at Springfield's Lanphier Park. Mayor Buddy Kapp stepped in to play catcher that day.

Springfield Sallies

Sallies' catcher, Zonia Vialet, waits for the pitch as batter Jan Marlowe of the Kenosha team takes a practice swing. The ten league teams in 1948 were all headquartered in Midwest towns, but the players came from all across the U.S., Canada, and even Cuba.

Women have played baseball since the late 1860s, and some were even playing professionally, but history has given them scant notice. A little-known fact is that Springfield had the country's first salaried women baseball players–the Blondes and Brunettes. From 1875 into the mid-1880s, they entertained crowds across the country. The women played more as entertainers than as professionals. It wasn't until after World War II that Springfield again had a women's team of salaried players. This time they were professional athletes. J.R. "Bud" Fitzpatrick was granted the tenth franchise in 1948 for an All-American Girls Base Ball League (1943-1954) team, the first and only women's league. The Springfield Sallies won their opening game on May 9, but within the month poor attendance made it obvious Springfield would not support a women's team. The Sallies then became a traveling team and folded altogether in 1949.

Lady-like behavior was expected by the league of women athletes. No shorts or slacks were to be worn in public, hair was to be kept long, and proper make-up was to be worn even when on the baseball field. The Sallies' chaperon was Springfield native and all-round athlete, Mary Rudis.

The Springfield Sallies' emblem with its Abraham Lincoln profile can be seen on Ruby Stephens' uniform as she runs the bases at the Fitzpatrick Memorial Stadium, located in the 2700 block of South Fourth Street.

Springfield Sports Hall of Fame

The Springfield Sports Hall of Fame was organized in 1991 to honor some of the outstanding athletes the city has produced over the years. The members of the Hall represent the wide diversity of sports played in the city–baseball, football, basketball, and golf, to name a few. Sixty-nine athletes have been inducted so far.

Springfield Sports Hall of Fame Members

1991

Al Barlick–National League baseball umpire 1940-71. Named to Baseball Hall of Fame, Cooperstown, New York, 1989.

Dick Boushka–Basketball player for St. Louis University and 1956 United States Olympic basketball team, which captured the gold medal.

Ron Gibbs–professional football official for 23 years, including 15 Super Bowl games.

Jimmy Johnson–Springfield High School and Illinois State Normal University track star. Tied world records in the 100-yard and 220-yard dashes.

Josh Johnson–played in the Negro National and American professional leagues from 1934-1942.

Dr. Stan London–Lead scorer in city basketball in 1943, competed and coached in college basketball and baseball and team physician for St. Louis Cardinals.

Jake Moore–One of the best bowlers in Springfield's history, with a career spanning 50 years.

Mark Peterman–Springfield High School basketball coach from 1929 to 1948, with 317 victories and a state championship team in 1935.

Ray Ramsey–3-sport athlete at Bradley University, played 10 years of professional football and two seasons in NBA. Also coached track at Lanphier High School.

Robin Roberts–Professional baseball pitcher from 1948 to 1966 with a career record of 286-245.

Dave Robisch–Outstanding Springfield High School basketball star and professional basketball player for 13 seasons.

John Shaive–professional baseball player of 15 years including five seasons in the major leagues.

Elaine Scheffler–Springfield bowler who won a record 10 Round-The-Town Tournament titles and 27 singles, doubles and team titles in the Springfield Women's Bowling Association Tournament.

Herb Scheffler–Star for Springfield High School's 1935 championship basketball team. Played college and professional basketball. Coached Springfield High School team from 1949 to 1955.

Robin Roberts appears at left with New York Yankee's pitching great, Whitey Ford.

Rex Easton, at right, shaking hands with Secretary of State Charles Carpenter.

Dick Schofield–played for 7 major league baseball teams during 19 years.

Ducky Schofield–Professional baseball player for 11 years and high school football and basketball referee for 10 years.

Ed Sternaman–Springfield High School football and basketball star. Was a partner with George Halas in forming the Chicago Bears in 1921.

Joe Sternaman–all-state quarterback for Springfield High School, played for University of Illinois, and was involved with Chicago Bears organization.

Billy Stone–Lanphier High School athlete and professional football player. Head football coach at Bradley University for 15 years.

Otto Stowe–Former Miami Dolphins and Dallas Cowboys' football player, later a fitness trainer and sports counselor.

Bob Trumpy–All-state high school football and basketball player, 1963 long jump state champion, and professional football player for 10 seasons.

Al Urbanckas– State high-jump title winner in 1954 and NCAA co-champion, Big Ten conference record-holder in 1957.

Kim Schofield Werth–Winner of 7 state track and high-jump titles while at Southeast High School.

Chuck Weyant–Auto racer with 4 Indianapolis appearances and several midget and sprint car wins.

1992

Don Casper–played 3 sports for Springfield High School, went on to play one year at University of Illinois.

Bob Charlton–winner of a record 6 Men's City Amateur Championships and head professional of Lincoln Greens for 18 years.

Tom Cole–Player on 1959 Springfield High School state basketball championship team and later for University of Michigan.

Roger Erickson–major league baseball pitcher and pitching coach for the Springfield Cardinals.

John Knight–winner of 3 consecutive Men's City Amateur titles. Later turned professional.

Jim Kopatz - talented 3-sport athlete, quarterback for the University of Illinois and drafted by 3 major league baseball teams.

Arlyn Lober–winningest Springfield High School basketball coach with 372 victories.

Herb McMath–played 2 years of professional football for the Oakland Raiders and Greenbay Packers. Won a Superbowl ring in 1977.

Fred Myers–played for the St. Louis Cardinals and managed the team one year.

Paul Reynolds–outstanding football player for Cathedral High School. Played for Notre Dame before being injured.

Bill Roellig–All-time winningest football coach in Springfield history. Coached Springfield High School football 1929-1953.

1993

Mary Rudis Bestudik–Center and point guard on the St. Louis American Legion basketball team that finished second in the 1934 AAU national tournament. Also a skilled bowler.

Johnnie Brittin–Professional baseball player for the Philadelphia Phillies for 2 seasons.

Rex Easton–Winner of 3 major auto-racing championships and other titles in the Midwest including the Illinois Auto Racing Association championship in 1947.

Don Erickson–Professional baseball pitcher for 12 years including a stint with the Philadelphia Phillies.

Judi Meador–Winner of a record 11 Women's City Golf Tournament championships.

Eddie Page–a dominant Springfield bowler in the 1950s and 1960s, as well as the holder of several national bowling titles.

Ray Page–Springfield High School basketball coach with several state tournament appearances. Won the state championship in 1959 with a team record of 33-1.

Al Papal–Pitcher who won 190 games during his professional career.

Bill Reynolds–Cathedral High School football standout and professional football player.

Dick Tate–Lettered in football and baseball at Illinois State University. First African-American to captain an ISU varsity team. Later played professional baseball and semi-pro football.

1994

Hal Edwards–Fast-pitch softball and minor league baseball player who also played golf and tennis.

Pat Kane–Talented baseball player who played on 4 teams that made it to the American Baseball Congress National Tournament in Battle Creek, Michigan.

Ron Little–Lanphier High School athlete selected to All-City teams in football, basketball, and baseball.

Arlyn Lober

Ray Page

Bill Roellig

John O'Connor–Boxer and sports promoter, winner of the featherweight boxing crown in 1894.

Jim Rockford played football for Griffin High School, University of Oklahoma Sooners, and American and Canadian football leagues.

Lynn Callahan Ruppert– Scored a record 48 points in 1977 Girls City Tournament and averaged 27.6 points a game as a senior.

Dale Schofield–Only Springfield golfer to win 5 Men's City Tournaments in succession. Later became a Springfield Park District professional player.

Larry Selinger–Lettered 3 years in football and 2 in basketball for Griffin High School. Played 4 years as starting quarterback for Bradley University. Later coached basketball at Griffin.

Eddie Sommers–Football and basketball player for Cathedral High School, football and baseball for Bradley University, and on several amateur baseball and basketball teams.

1995

Ted Boyle–coached baseball at Lanphier High School for 17 years without a losing season.

Toy Dorgan–1968 Winter Olympics speedskater.

Rudy Favero–Top athlete at Lanphier High School during 1940s and 1950s. Played for Boston Red Sox organization two years.

Alby Plain–Springfield High School athlete, played for University of Illinois and Chicago Cubs. Later coached at Springfield High School.

Kelly Ryan–Quarterbacked for Griffin High School and Yale University, setting several school passing records while at Yale.

Bob Zanot–Multisport athlete at Griffin High School known especially for football accomplishments.

1996

Jim Belz–Coach at Cathedral Boys High School and professional baseball player with the St. Louis Cardinals.

Ed Charlton–Co-record holder of 6 Men's City Golf tournament titles along with his brother, Bobby. Excellent bowler and member of the Greater Springfield Bowling Association Hall of Fame.

Allen Crowe–One of the top U.S. race car drivers of his time.

Walt David–Accomplished amateur baseball and basketball player.

Harry Eielson–Excellent basketball player and pole vaulter for Springfield High School.

Jim Potter–4-sport athlete for Southeast High School and Bradley University track star.

Ducky Reed–Long-time fast-pitch softball pitcher.

Marek Schaive–Semi-pro baseball player for 23 years with 2 seasons in minor leagues.

Marge Tapocik–One of the city's all-time top female athletes.

Teams

1935 Springfield High School Boys Basketball Team
1964 Griffin High School Boys Baseball Team
1959 Springfield High School Boys Basketball Team
1917 Springfield High School Boys Basketball Team
1973 Southeast High School Girls Track Team

Marge Tapocik

Jimmy Johnson

Ducky Reed

Marek Schaive

Walt David

Allen Crowe

Jim Potter

147

Leigh Day, 1861-1910. Mrs. Leigh (Gross) Day was a talented Springfield artist who began experimenting with photography about 1900. She posed her children for photographs, which she then used for sketching models. Those photos were charming enough in themselves to form illustrations for the original children's stories she wrote, which appeared in national magazines. The success of these stories led her to publish two children's books, *In Shadowland* and *Borderland and the Blue Beyond*. Many of the scenes in these books were taken in her own garden or those of her friends, including neighbor Susan Lawrence Dana. Her untimely death at age forty-nine in 1910 ended a promising career.

Henry B. House, 1877-1953. Although employed in banking for a large part of his life, Henry House's heart was in the theater. Around the age of twenty-six he left a banking position in Springfield to become the private secretary and treasurer to the famed Shakespearian actor, Richard Mansfield. Upon returning to Springfield in 1921, he founded the Community Players and served as its director for ten years. In 1934 he helped organize the Little Theater, which existed from 1934 to 1939. House's credits include the directing of plays for theatrical groups in other towns as well as acting and writing original scripts. He also wrote and gave talks about theater history.

Virginia S. Eifert, 1911-1966. Author Virginia (Snider) Eifert's ability to use adjectives and metaphors when writing about nature gave her readers many vivid mental pictures. The award-winning author wrote eighteen books and numerous articles. She was also passionately interested in American history. Her first books were a series for children about Abraham Lincoln. Her articles appeared in *Audubon*, *Natural History,* and *Nature*. In 1939 she began her career as editor of the Illinois State Museum's *Living Museum*. The Springfield native was a talented artist and photographer, illustrating many of her works.

John Carroll Power, 1819-1894. It wasn't until well into his fifties that John Carroll Power began to pursue writing on a professional level. He was brought up as a Virginia farmer with a very limited education. He had, though, a strong desire to learn and the assistance he needed from his wife, Sarah. Power published several books and wrote for magazines before he gave up farming for good. In 1869 he made Springfield his home. His *Life of Lincoln* was well received by the public and his *An Attempt to Steal the Body of Lincoln* has become a primary resource for scholars. Most used, however, is his invaluable *The Early Settlers of Sangamon County*, which documents families living in Sangamon County before 1850. From 1873 until his death, he was the custodian at the Lincoln Tomb, a position that called for the expertise of a historian.

Nicholas Vachel Lindsay, 1879-1931. Of Springfield-born writers, Vachel Lindsay was the most celebrated in the United States and England. His new poetry captured the American imagination from 1913 to the early 1920s. Lindsay began his professional career as an artist and taught in New York City. Soon, though, his compulsion to express his ideas and philosophy for a better society turned him to poetry and prose. Ordinary people, he felt, could make a difference and he literally "tramped" across the United States trading his poetry and drawings to pay for meals. The rhythm found in his poetry was designed so that everyone, not just intellectuals, would be attracted to his works. Lindsay also worked as a newspaper columnist and lecturer, and he was involved in a number of civic projects, tirelessly promoting the weaving of artistic sensibility into everyday life and work.

Charles Leonard Skelton, 1890-1957. *Riding West on the Pony Express* was a juvenile western written by Charles Skelton that sold over 25,000 copies in the United States and in England. Skelton, whose lifelong desire was to be recognized as an author, was originally from Toluca, Illinois. The West intrigued him and so after college he headed in that direction. A bout with polio and then the start of the Great Depression brought him back to Illinois. He found work under Secretary of State William Stratton. A change of politics in 1933 put him out of work and he turned writing into a full-time career. Initially he sold serialized short stories and later returned to government and worked as a writer for Governor William Stratton, son of the former Secretary of State.

Skip Farrell, ca. 1919-1962. Charles F. Fielder, was better known to his Springfield High School classmates as "Skip," or "Farrell." He began a professional singing career as Skip Farrell and was touted by the *Chicago Tribune* in 1945 as having "one of the finest voices this side of Crosby, infinitely better than Sinatra." Farrell became a starring singer on Chicago's WMAQ evening program and made regular appearances on other radio spots as well. He headlined with bands at nightclubs, dinner dances, and parties. Farrell recorded two successful releases for Capitol Records and was sent off to Hollywood to make more. Farrell is one of many talented singers, musicians, and actors that Springfield has produced. Some stayed in town to share their talents with local theater groups, symphonies, and choirs, while others turned professional.

Hiram E. Jackson. Jr., ca. 1910-1978. Hiram E. Jackson Jr. was the first African-American staff artist for the *Illinois State Journal* and *Illinois State Register* newspapers. Jackson's award-winning paintings gave him fame beyond Springfield. Two were chosen as permanent hangings at the Art Institute in Minneapolis, Minnesota, and a third hangs at Lincoln University in Jefferson, Missouri, where Jackson graduated. Born in Greenville, Mississippi, Jackson came to Springfield as a child in 1922 and made his home here, until he was transferred to the Copley Press office in San Diego in 1963.

Carl G. Hodges, 1902-1964. A good crime story became the trademark of the prolific writer Carl G. Hodges, newspaper columnist, radio commentator, and public relations head at the Illinois Information Service. He wrote countless magazine stories in the hard-boiled, pulp-fiction tradition and published five book-length detective stories and twenty novelettes. His interviews and articles covered a wide range of topics. A desire to teach led him to write several books he called "painless history" for children, stories set in historically accurate settings. Originally from Quincy, Hodges made Springfield his home from 1942 until his death.

E. Carl Lundgren, ca. 1898-1974. E. Carl Lundgren dreamed of Springfield as a music and cultural center and dedicated his life's work to that end. He came to Springfield in 1928 as the music director at Springfield High School and at First Christian Church. With the assistance of his wife, Alma Abbott Lundgren of Springfield, he became founding director of the Springfield Municipal Choir, which he led until his death. The Lundgrens also founded the Illinois Wesleyan Junior College of Music in Springfield, which existed for seventeen years, and the 'old' Muni Opera in 1950. He remained active with the 'new' Muni when it reorganized in 1964.

William Wallace Grieves, 1894-1989. For twenty-one years Wallace Grieves delighted concertgoers with a mixture of classical and lighter, popular selections as he conducted the Springfield Civic Orchestra. Grieves was born in Lacon, Illinois. He began his career as a violinist, teaching at Millikin University in Decatur and Illinois Wesleyan College in Bloomington. In 1915 he came to Springfield and co-founded, with Clarence Mayer, the Springfield College of Music and Allied Arts, a certified college offering a bachelors degree in music. The school, at its peak, had 400 students and 14 instructors.  The students from the college gave impetus to the founding of the Civic Orchestra in 1921. The school closed and Grieves moved on to other teaching positions when financial support for the orchestra was no longer sufficient. Activity was suspended in 1941. He died in 1989 at age 95.

Benjamin P. Thomas, 1902-1956. New Jersey-born author, editor, insurance agent, and cattleman Benjamin P. Thomas came to Springfield in 1932 as the executive secretary of the Abraham Lincoln Association. He gained a national reputation as a Lincoln scholar. After some twenty years of research and writing on Lincoln and related topics, he published the biography (1952) simply called *Abraham Lincoln*. This definitive work became a best seller and set a new standard for Lincoln biographies. It made use of new information and portrayed Lincoln as a human with character flaws and strengths.

Cal Shrum, 1910-1996. "Singing cowboy" Cal Shrum began his career with a western band. He was born in Arkansas but married singer Mary Frances Wise, from near Williamsville, Illinois, in 1941. Shrum, with his wife, whose professional name was Alta Lee, made records and co-starred in fourteen western movies. He totaled fifty-nine westerns in all, including some with Gene Autry and Roy Rogers. His "Heaven Bound Train" recording is in the Country Music Hall of Fame. From 1950 to 1964 Shrum was a popular WMAY radio personality.

William Dodd Chenery, 1860-1942. William Dodd Chenery was a master at planning pageants, including scripting, staging, music arrangements and even costume design. His *Egypta* (1891) was in production seventeen years and often had as many as 2,000 participants, depending on where it was performed. Chenery wrote pageants for building dedications, centennial celebrations, and chatauquas throughout the U.S. Though he rarely composed original music, his wide knowledge of classical music was put to use in creating the Biblical and historical dramas for which he was famous. Springfield's "musical missionary" was a leading force in the formation of the Springfield Civic Orchestra, Municipal Band, and Municipal Chorus.

Louis Lehmann, 1851-1923. Among Springfield musicians who put their heart and soul into music, Professor Louis Lehmann must be among the top. German born, he immigrated to the United States in 1866. He first visited Springfield to conduct The German Reed Band for two months in 1878. He returned permanently in 1881 to head the Illinois Watch Factory Band. The band was a regular in the 1900s at the Sunday afternoon concerts held in Lincoln and Washington parks and at dances held in the pavilions. Lehmann gave vocal, piano, and violin lessons to many as well as being organist in several of the churches in Springfield. His wife, a soprano soloist, often worked with her husband on church services. The bandstand in Washington Park was erected in his memory.

Lillian Scalzo, 1900-1984. It is said of Lillian Scalzo that she made Springfield "art conscious." While working to master the piano and the violin at age eighteen, she took an art course and discovered another talent. From then she devoted much of her time to developing her skills and natural talent in a wide variety of mediums—watercolor, sculpture, oil painting, etchings, lithographs, ceramics, stitchery, and her favorite—copper enameling. Scalzo, a Springfield native, enthusiastically shared what she learned. In 1929 she organized the art department at Springfield Junior College (now Springfield College in Illinois). In 1933 she became the first and for a time, only instructor at the Springfield Art Association. Her joy in creating was contagious to all those who had contact with her.

The Muni Opera's theater at Lake Springfield has entertained thousands of central Illinoisans. First opened in 1950, the Muni was reborn in 1964 after a rocky financial history. A surprising number of talented Springfield actors has brought favorite Broadway productions to life summer after summer. Two of the more popular during the 1970s were, *1776* (top photo) and *Most Happy Fella*.

Cars ...

With the coming of the automobile families had a whole new way to entertain themselves—the Sunday ride. This Springfield family takes an outing in the country about 1915. Husband and baby in the front are joined by wife and perhaps a mother-in-law in the backseat.

Springfieldians quickly adapted their cars to special uses, camping, for instance. Companies sold specialty accessories like these auto tents, which folded out and made anywhere the car stopped an instant campground.

Car shows such as this one at the state arsenal in 1927 provided Springfield residents an opportunity to compare the latest models and to pick the one best suited to their needs and, more importantly, their pocketbooks. Some of these new, polished automobiles bear names of manufacturers no longer in existence—Whippett, Willys-Knight, and Nash. Others such as Ford, Dodge, and Buick remain well-known to this day.

On July 1, 1914, five dentists, including Thomas Donelan of Springfield, began a road trip to New York. In those early days of automobile travel the men experienced "high adventure" on the open road. When they returned home one of them wrote up a record of the trip and had presentation copies printed, giving it the title: "The Official Log of the Order of the Knights of the Greasy Vest and Dirty Shirt." Shown at Gettysburg, Pennsylvania, are left to right: W.F. Whalen, Thomas Donelan, Charles L. Snyder, Henry L. Whipple, and E.F. Hazell.

The 1950s may have been the high point of lavish design and innovation in American cars. Yearly style changes were dramatic and eagerly awaited by the public. The grand failure, symbolic of that era, was Ford's Edsel. Months of pent-up curiosity preceeded the September 4, 1957, unveiling of Ford Motor Company's totally new car—"E-Day" according to company publications. A "small mob" of curious seekers surround the first Edsel in town, parked at Fifth and Monroe streets.

For generations a teen-age rite-of-passage has been qualifying for a driver's license. Driver education classes were an important part of Springfield Public School curriculum by the 1950s. Here Springfield High School instructor Roger Kendall guides a young man through driving maneuvers in 1961. The driver's license was a ticket to adventure and independence for countless Springfield teens during the 1950s and '60s "drive-in" era.

Springfield, was fascinated, and still is, with cars. Private auto ownership went from a few in 1900 to several hundred in the 1920s. For a short time in 1910 there was even a automobile made here by the Rayfield Motor Company, named appropriately, "The Springfield." In this 1910 photo of a "Springfield" test drive are some well-known Springfield men: Howard and Homer Welch, Clarence W. Chiles, John Workman, John W. Hobbs, Harry Loper, Ernest Mayhew, and Herbert Georg.

Endurance runs were popular public relations events in early auto days. Local dealers hosted drivers and their cars in cross-country runs to demonstrate reliability. In some cases dealers sponsored their own runs like Springfield's Elliott Van Brunt Oakland dealership. For 172 hours this car's engine ran continously as crowds and reporters turned out to view the results. This view from about 1917 is taken in front of the dealership at 315 East Adams Street.

Henry Ford's Model T put America on wheels. Statistics during the 1920s showed more Americans owned cars than bathtubs. Women drivers became very common during the decade and housewives or young unmarried women found new independence with their own transportation. Here a Springfield woman poses proudly with her Model T. Although a hand crank is visible, the car may have had an automatic starter.

Presidential Limos

Springfield residents always turn out in large numbers for the visit of a U.S. President—current or past. A special part of any presidential visit is a motorcade through downtown Springfield. These views are typical from Springfield presidential visitors through the years.

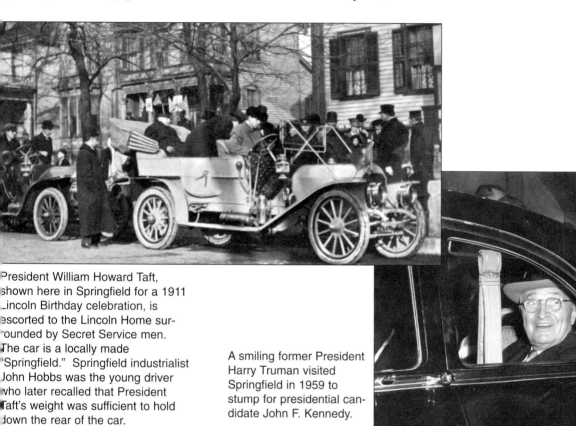

President William Howard Taft, shown here in Springfield for a 1911 Lincoln Birthday celebration, is escorted to the Lincoln Home surrounded by Secret Service men. The car is a locally made "Springfield." Springfield industrialist John Hobbs was the young driver who later recalled that President Taft's weight was sufficient to hold down the rear of the car.

A smiling former President Harry Truman visited Springfield in 1959 to stump for presidential candidate John F. Kennedy.

President John F. Kennedy arrives at Capital Airport and is chauffeured in a trademark Lincoln Continental convertible. At right is then-Illinois Governor Otto Kerner.

Acknowledgements

All of the photographs in this book were taken from Lincoln Library's Sangamon Valley Collection. We would especially like to thank individuals who provided photos to be copied for the Collection so that they could appear in the book. These include:

Carlin Baker
R. Lou Barker
Mrs. Kenneth Barton
Robert Becker
Betsy Burton
Mrs. Ray Capella
Bertha Cochran
Gloria Cohen
Robert Corey
Nancy Drake
Ed Eck

Jean Fisherkeller
Minette Fuhrman
Mrs. James Galloway
Eugene Hanson
Richard E. Hart
Jim Helm
Don Hickman
Craig Isbell
Dennis Kerasotes
George and Hilda Kidd
Aden Lauchner

Mary Maggenti
Mrs. William Menghini
Grace Luttrell Nanavanti
Dudley J. O'Neil
James Patton
Richard W. Phillips
H. Wayne Price
Ron Reynolds
James Rollett
Keith Sculle
Homer Sharp

Nancy Spinner
Springfield Muni Opera
State Journal-Register
Mike Troesch
Dorothy Wallace
WICS-Channel 20
James Woodruff

This book could not have existed except for the dozens of photographers—professional and amateur—who took the pictures. To them we are sincerely grateful and apologize to any contributors we might have failed to mention.

Bibliography

Angle, Paul M. *Here I Have Lived. A History of Lincoln's Springfield, 1831-1865.* Springfield, Illinois: Abraham Lincoln Association, 1935.

Annual Report of the Board of Trustees of the Pleasure Driveway and Park District. "Springfield, Illinois: Pleasure Driveway and Park District of Springfield," 1902.

Bateman, Newton, ed. *Historical Encyclopedia of Illinois* and *History of Sangamon County.* Chicago: Munsell, 1912.

Buley, R. Carlyle. *The Old Northwest Pioneer Period 1815-1840.* Indianapolis: Indiana Historical Society, 1950.

Cook, John C. *Reminiscences of Springfield.* Springfield, Illinois: *Illinois State Journal*, 1927.

Dulles, Foster Rhea. *A History of Recreation.* New York: Meredith Publishing Company, 1965.

Hayes, John G. *A History of The Springfield Symphony Orchestra.* Springfield, Illinois: J. G. Hayes, 1993.

Inter-State Publishing Company. *History of Sangamon County, Illinois.* Chicago: Inter-State Publishing Company, 1881.

Karban, Roger. Dirt. *Belleville, Illinois:* Stellar Publications, 1984.

Sangamon Valley Collection. Vertical Files. Springfield, Illinois, Lincoln Library.

Springfield City Directory. Springfield, Illinois: R.L. Polk & Co. Numerous years were consulted in the writing of this book.

Springfield in Eighteen Ninety-Six. Springfield, Illinois: *Illinois State Journal*, 1896.

Index

National City Bank
wishes to dedicate this
publication to the
people of Springfield,
past and present,
who with vision and
determination have created
our vibrant community.